THE NATION HOLDS ITS BREATH
GREAT IRISH SOCCER QUOTATIONS

Eoghan Corry is a columnist and sometime sports editor, and the author of more sports books than is safe to mention in polite society. The record he established at Clane under-14s for the number of own goals by one player in a single match still stands.

THE NATION HOLDS ITS BREATH

Great Irish Soccer Quotations

Eoghan Corry

HODDER
HEADLINE
IRELAND

A CIP catalogue record for this title is available from
the British Library.

ISBN 0340 92152 8

Typeset in Berling Antiqua and Schindler by Hodder Headline Ireland
Printed and bound in Great Britain by Clays Ltd, St Ives plc.

Hodder Headline's policy is to use papers that are natural, renewable
and recyclable products and made from wood grown in sustainable
forests. The logging and manufacturing processes are expected to
conform to the environmental regulations of the country of origin.

Hodder Headline Ireland
8 Castlecourt Centre, Castleknock, Dublin 15, Ireland

A division of Hodder Headline
338 Euston Road, London NW1 3BH

Contents

For Cillian

And all who play, cheer or wave a flag in hope

For my own favourite soccer panel: David, Páraic, Stephen, Fergal, Richard, Ann, Rebecca, Karen, Connie, Daniel, Harry, Alexander, Síofra, Bill, Sebastian, Aoife, John and Saoirse.

And in memory of my Uncle Jack
John Corry RIP
Who brought me to my first big match in Highbury in August 1973 and changed my life.

Introduction

'There is a tide in the affairs of men, which, taken at the flood, leads on to fortune.' True, so true. That was one of the very first teamtalks, Brutus catching the essence of the moment to rouse his men for the big game against Julius Caesar. Just one thing – they weren't his words, they were Shakespeare's.

Down through the ages, politicians, princes of public affairs, knights of commerce, captains of industry – whenever they've had something to say, they've had someone to script it.

Not so in sport. Spontaneity is its very essence. You can no more script a sporting event than you can, with certainty, entwine your two weeks of summer vacation with the warmest of an Irish summer. So it's hardly any wonder that the words of those who are privileged to annotate the action with their commentary, and those whose privilege has been the participation in it, should sometimes leave a mark that wasn't quite what they intended.

I make this observation as one who has been proven – statistically, apparently – to have been responsible for around 87 per cent of the goals conceded by the Republic of Ireland over twenty years or so through injudicious chicken counting.

Hence, that summer's evening in Hanover during Euro '88, when Ireland, fresh from their historic win over England the previous weekend, were 1–0 up against the Soviet Union with a quarter of an hour to go, and that fabled goalkeeper, Packie Bonner, was entitled to expect another clean sheet. The innocent remark, 'Bonner has gone 165 minutes of this tournament without conceding a goal – he's heading for his ninth consecutive shut-out', begun when play was deep in opposition territory, suddenly morphed into the transfixed shriek of 'Danger here!' For, in those few seconds, the ball travelled over half the length of the pitch to land at the feet of Oleg Protasov. He promptly dispatched it beyond Bonner's reach into the Irish net. Ouch!

But then, that's live broadcasting. No more than the player who misses the sitter, circumstance lies in wait for the commentator. Many of the gems within these covers were uttered by folk who'd have expressed themselves better had they had the opportunity, like the best of scriptwriters, to sit down at a desk and reflect. But the delight is in the dissemination of instant information, which is carried by the might of the moment. The mirth that ensues is of no harm to the perpetrator – it's all part of the game.

Sometimes we get it right. No one who witnessed Kevin Keegan's mid-90s tirade as he contemplated the prospect of usurping Manchester United's position of pre-eminence in the Premiership – 'I would love it, just love it' – when he was manager of Newcastle would doubt that some of the best scripts are unwritten and unrehearsed.

Equally, the BBC commentator Kenneth Wolstenholme's reaction to the minor pitch invasion at the end of the 1966 World Cup final is in the annals. England were leading West Germany 3–2, extra-time was almost over. As England swept forward for one last assault, a couple of fans lost the run of themselves. In the days before steel fences and mass stewarding, the playing field was wide open. They burst out of the stands to cavort in celebration, as Geoff Hurst, who'd scored twice already, set off towards the German goal. Wolstenholme never broke stride. 'Some people are on the pitch,' he observed with as much calm as he could muster. 'They think it's all over!' Hurst's shot hit the net. 'It is now!'

'They think it's all over' entered the English vernacular. We have lots of examples of our own and I am both delighted and honoured that Eoghan should have chosen one of mine for the title of his book.

'The nation holds its breath' is something I said one day many years ago. I happened to be on the air. It was a last sixteen match in the 1990 World Cup finals in Italy. Tom Flanagan, my RTÉ sidekick, had been with me through Sardinia and Sicily, and now our Cook's Tour of Italy was bringing us by car to Genoa.

We set off from Milan that Monday morning, stopping at a wine shop before we got to the autostrada. It was possible Ireland might beat Romania, and reaching the World Cup quarter-finals would merit champagne. The sunny drive south was a delight, team-mates sharing the trip with a boistrous reflection on three weeks following the football.

Back home it was a big day. Ireland was ending its six-month presidency of the European Union. In Dublin Castle, they were about to crown the summit. In Genoa, Tom and I were smuggling champagne, for – never mind alcohol – bottles were not permitted inside those World Cup stadia.

The football game was forgettable, and ending 0–0 was no solution. There had to be extra time. As it wore on to its inevitable conclusion, the heads of government were assembling to pay public tribute to Ireland's six-month stewardship of the EU.

Then rang the Angelus bell. And, on RTÉ1, the *Six-One News* began.

'Ireland's presidency of the European Union is concluding with a press conference at Dublin Castle. Ireland's World Cup effort has reached stalemate – scoreless after extra-time. There will be a penalty shootout.'

In Genoa, Packie Bonner makes a save which means that if Ireland score with the next kick, they're in the quarter-finals.

In Dublin Castle, the press conference is suspended as The Taoiseach – Charles Haughey – announces there is something very important to which we should attend first. Eyes turn to the television.

All of Europe awaits. And inhales. And, in Genoa, as David O'Leary places the ball on the penalty spot, and steps back to eyeball the Romanian goalkeeper and work out how he's going to match his team-mate's stunning save, the guy with the bottle of champagne in his satchel does what he has to do, and makes a comment, 'The nation holds its breath.'

O'Leary shoots, the net bulges, the commentator yelps… and Ireland is in the last eight in the world!

The story concludes in the interview room after the match. Flanagan and Hamilton have smuggled the champagne all the way there but, after the hours spent in the boot of a travelling car on an afternoon in the Italian high summer, followed by the couple of hours in the commentary box, it isn't exactly fresh when it's presented in celebration to the two key participants – Bonner and O'Leary – live on RTÉ Television. It's the temperature of builder's tea. They take one sip, disapprove, then disgorge the lot over the head of the interviewer, yours truly, live on air.

There's a story behind every quotation within these covers. My hope is that imagining what it might be will enhance your enjoyment. And I commend Eoghan Corry wholeheartedly for bringing it all together.

GEORGE HAMILTON
February 2006

Prologue

'They do not play often at football, only in a small territory called Fingal near Dublin where the people use it much, and trip and shoulder very handsomely.'

John Dunton, describing football in Ireland during his travels in 1698-99, *The Life and Errors of John Dunton, Citizen of London* (1818).

It was an Irishman, Oscar Wilde, who gave us the original soccer soundbyte when he said rugby football was 'a savage's game played by gentlemen' and that association football was 'a gentlemen's game played by savages'.

Another Irishman, George Best, fuelled an entire soccer quotation industry with his comments on women, drink and squandered money and helped inspire a series of books of collected soccer wisdom that has grown and flourished ever since.

As Best's career went into premature tailspin, a third Irishman, Eamon Dunphy, wrote the most significant book about the game by a soccer player, proving that footballers did have something interesting to say if they got the chance.

These three gentlemen transformed life for those of us who love collecting the utterances of sportsmen, the footlore of the beautiful game.

Until Best arrived and pushed soccer on to the front pages of newspapers instead of the back, and until Dunphy's *Only a Game* was published, it was assumed that players had nothing interesting to say – and maybe that was because people took Wilde too literally.

In those days, it was unusual for journalists to talk to a player after a match and, even if they did, the quotes were banal and often made up.

The system worked like this: 'Is this the happiest day of your life?' 'Yes.'

And this became 'It was the happiest day of my life' for the morning paper.

That approach changed when players like Best became household names for people who never followed sport and began to get to say something away from the locker-room environment. Soccer forgot its past and emerged, blinking into a new world of live television, intelligent post-match analysis and literary journalists who wrote heavily stylised essays about the events that had happened within the confines of space and time that represent a soccer match.

At which point we meet Dunphy again, determined to turn the studio analysis of games into something as entertaining as anything on the sports field and succeeding, after the 1984 European Championship, in establishing the reputation of Ireland's studio team as one of the best in Europe.

By the time the 2006 World Cup came around, every studio in Dublin, London, Madrid and New York seemed to have a loquacious ex-Irish international on its panel.

The quotations industry has been augmented, sometimes inadvertently, by commentators with more live television time to kill, endless analysis by former players, and kiss-and-tell revelations in the newspapers, often scripted by literate collaborators.

By the early 1980s, newspapers like the *Sunday Tribune* were running 'Sports quotes of the week' columns and the first collections of soccer quotations were being released on the English market by the *Tribune*'s soccer correspondent (and Dunphy's *Only a Game* collaborator) Peter Ball – a development that might even have changed the way players and managers talked about the game.

By the time Mick McCarthy had left the job of managing the Irish team, he was delivering an assembly line of witticisms that kept Monday morning columnists and webloggers in business, and will no doubt continue to do so whichever lonely touchline he decides to furrow in the future.

Broadcasting commentaries in themselves gave rise to a cottage industry and the Irish commentators even began to challenge David Coleman's stature of the inventor of another genre – the gaffe.

The sports memoir too has taken on a new life too, with the publication of Andy Townsend's, Tony Cascarino's and Niall Quinn's collaborative memoirs with journalists Paul Kimmage and Tom Humphries.

The memoir entered a new phase when Roy Keane was suspended, not for the tackle he made on Alf-Inge Haaland in 2001, but for his description of the same tackle he made when his biography (co-written by Dunphy) appeared nearly two years later.

While Ireland may never have won the World Cup for their deeds on the field, they are real contenders when it comes to talking about it. What follows is a modest tribute to the way Irish players and supporters have changed the way we watch one of our favourite games, and certainly the way we talk about it.

EOGHAN CORRY
January 2006

All in a Game

It is extraordinary how much that is said and written about football is not about the game at all. Somewhere at the heart of all the debate, the rows, the nostalgia, the guff, the passion and the emotion, there are people trying to kick a sack of wind around the field.

'Football is all very well as a game for rough girls, but it is hardly suitable for delicate boys.'

Oscar Wilde.

'Men trifle with their business and their politics but never trifle with their games. They cannot pretend that they have won when they have lost.'

George Bernard Shaw.

'Soccer is the most democratic of all field games in that it has room for the big and the small and for those who are not particularly gifted with basic speed.'

Con Houlihan (May 1989).

'The man in charge of our wolf cubs teams in Belfast was not a coach, but he loved football. On Sunday mornings, he would read out the match reports of the previous day's games. He made football a romance and, above all else, that is what the game should be.'

Danny Blanchflower (1983).

'Is this really what football at international level has come down to? Guys who are big and strong motoring up and down the pitch. Is this the beautiful game? Is this the glory game? I could get on the Greece team. I've played with guys like that. I don't want to see them picking up a cup.'

Eamon Dunphy, talking after Euro 2004.

'After the joy of hammering a burst ball against a wall, the only surprises life had left for him were sex and Elvis.'

Roddy Doyle, watching his son Rory grow up.

'I loved soccer. I still love it. If I didn't I couldn't tolerate the way people treat me inside the game.'

Danny Blanchflower, quoted in *The Encyclopaedia of Association Football* (1960).

'Two visits to Terryland Park gave me my fill of soccer. Bad Gaelic football and bad rugby football can bore me to the point when I say to myself, "Why don't these fellows find themselves a different game to play?" Bad soccer always forces me to ask myself, "Why don't these people give up?" This may be because the gap between good and bad is so wide in the case of the world's most popular ball game. Of course, these conclusions only arise when I am asked to pay to watch these activities. What consenting adults do to amuse themselves is an entirely different matter.'

Breandán Ó hEithir, *Over the Bar* (1984).

'The great fallacy is that the game is first and last about winning. It is nothing of the sort. The game is about glory. It is about doing things in style, with a flourish, about going out and beating the other lot, not waiting for them to die of boredom.'

Danny Blanchflower, quoted in Hunter Davies, *The Glory Game* (1972).

'Football is essentially a professional game but professional people are not allowed to run it. All the ideas are the prerogative of the butchers, bakers and candlestick makers; help is never sought from the players. When the international team is due to be selected, club managers, players and ex-players (in other words the only people qualified to be good judges of ability) must never interfere.'

Jimmy McIlroy, Northern Ireland international, *Right Inside Soccer* (1960).

'Soccer is run by second-rate conmen. Petit-bourgeois, frustrated small businessmen. It's a tragedy because socially football is very important.'

Eamon Dunphy (1973).

'The problem nowadays is that the kids have personal stereos and higher education.'
John Giles.

'Good captains, like dinosaurs, are threatened with extinction. They are being hounded into a state of nervous nonentity by a huge pack of master minds who inhabit the higher, drier lands of the grandstands.'
Danny Blanchflower, quoted in *The Encyclopaedia of Association Football* (1960).

Supporter: 'A fiver on Celtic to beat Arsenal.'
Bookie: 'I'm sorry sir, we don't take bets on friendlies.'
Supporter: 'Celtic dinnae play friendlies.'
Exchange in bookmaker's office before Arsenal v. Celtic testimonial (1980).

'We came out of school early, at 15, not the most educated people. In our early twenties, we are earning money that professional people are striving to earn in their forties. For all the good advice your dad can give, he doesn't know the ins and outs of contracts.'
Dave O'Leary (1993).

'You are inclined to take your habits into your life and into your game or your music or whatever it is. Now this is an age of violence. I think that our football is becoming violent. It seems that way to me.'
Danny Blanchflower, quoted in *The Encyclopaedia of Association Football* (1960).

'The beauty of soccer, the reason why I think it is the best team game of all, is that there are so many factors outside the control of the coach. If a coach could control a soccer game, it would become very boring indeed. In American football, the play becomes just an extension of the will and imagination of the two coaches. This can be fascinating, sure, but I'm not certain it has much to do with sport.'

John Giles, talking while he was the manager of the Vancouver Whitecaps (1984).

'I'd play for Ireland for nothing if they let everyone in for nothing. If they're collecting a fifty thousand gate, playing for hope and glory has nothing to do with the facts.'

Danny Blanchflower, quoted in *The Encyclopaedia of Association Football* (1960).

'Is there a carpenter in the ground?'

PA announcer at the FAI Cup semi-final between Finn Harps and Athlone Town, after goalkeeper Mick O'Brien broke the crossbar by swinging on it (1974).

'Today's players would leave us for dead. They deserve what money they can get.'

Johnny Carey, Manchester Utd and Ireland international 1937–53.

'Seven draws is an awful lot. If Bohs had won two or three of those and even lost the rest, they'd be in a wonderful position.'

Damien Richardson.

Battles and Riots

Ireland's reputation as one of the best behaved bunch of spectators in the game was acquired quite recently. The referee came within one minute of calling off the European Championship qualifier against Turkey in 1975 because of crowd violence. Early seventies soccer crowds liked to imitate the riots they saw on television from England. All that changed, largely thanks to a policy of self-policing devised by the Irish fans themselves.

Dublin's recent football riots have been associated with the visit of English supporters, such as those of Everton in 1985, the English national team in 1990 (skirmishing after the match led to a baton charge on Dublin's O'Connell Street), and the highest profile riot of all in 1995 when a group of English supporters caused a match between Ireland and England at Lansdowne Road to be abandoned.

Unsurprisingly, passions run highest among Belfast-based supporters when religion was involved. Cross-sectarian matches have led to gunfire at Belfast Celtic v. Linfield (1912) and Belfast Celtic v. Glentoran (1920), and more conventional stone-throwing at Linfield v. Cliftonville (1977), Linfield v. Dundalk (1979), Bohemians v. Glasgow Rangers (1983) and Donegall Celtic v. Linfield (1990). More unusual was Cliftonville v. Glasgow Celtic (1984), where the Northern Ireland police of the time, the RUC, were accused of fomenting a riot between two groups of nationalist/Catholic supporters.

'My team was composed of Catholics and Protestants. They mixed and they got on well together.'

Billy Bingham, on the Northern Ireland team that went to the 1982 and 1986 World Cup finals.

'A pity, because I won't get to jeer him on the field.'

Northern Ireland fan, being interviewed by RTÉ on the decision of Catholic player Neil Lennon not to continue playing for Northern Ireland because of a series of death threats (2002).

'We want to call the club after Glasgow Celtic and our aim is to imitate them in their style of play, win the Irish Cup, and follow their example in the cause of charity.'

Foundation meeting of Belfast Celtic (March 1891).

'All we hope for is a grand sporting game and, above all, may the best team win.'

Linfield v. Belfast Celtic match programme (27 December 1948). Anonymous letters and threats had been sent to Celtic Park warning Kevin McAlinden and Robin Lawler that they would be killed if they played.

'The scenes were the most disgraceful ever witnessed in connection with the Belfast football. Only one redeeming feature. Thanks to the energetic efforts of a band of Linfield stewards, the players were not interfered with, save that Wilgar received a blow of a stone on the head, which, however was not serious.'

Dublin newspaper, *Sport* (4 June 1919).

'The IFA are living in a fool's paradise if they fancy any Dublin team will travel to Belfast for the semi-final of the Irish Cup. They will travel to the final if they qualify, but not for the semi-final.'

Dublin newspaper, *Sport* (1920).

'Save for singing and flag-waving by a crowd of youths congregated underneath the reserved covering the match had been without incident up to ten minutes before the finish. The incident might have ended but for a fusillade of stone throwing from a section of the crowd at the unreserved exit.'

Report of a 1920 Glentoran v. Belfast Celtic match that ended with a revolver being discharged, *Irish News*.

'The disgrace that was brought on the Bohemian club last Saturday by a handful of young blackguards reinforced by the element to be found in all populous centres that is only too keen to take a prominent part in anything of the nature of a row, it is to be sincerely hoped will quickly be wiped out. Every decent-minded witness of the incident was thoroughly sickened and saddened by the spectacle and their full sympathy goes out to those who were actually deliberately assaulted. The referee Mr Coleton is badly injured notwithstanding his handling of the match to the outbreak of the blackguardism had been admirably impartial. Whether he should or should not have awarded a penalty against a Celtic back does not justify the crowd encroaching on the field of play and running amok. That is the concern of the teams not of the crowd.'

Dublin newspaper, *Sport* (13 September 1919).

'It just goes to prove the stupidity and futility of bigotry. I survived the "Jimmy Jones Incident", as people refer to it to this day, but, sadly, Belfast Celtic didn't survive and I hate to think they went into extinction because of what happened to me.

Jimmy Jones, talking in 1998 about 1948 game at Windsor Park where his leg was broken by an angry mob of Linfield fans. As a result of the attack the Belfast Celtic board declared that the team would never play in front of an Irish crowd again – and put all the players on the transfer list.

'They were kicking him up and down the terrace steps like a rag doll. Jimmy was screaming in pain and I could see his right leg was horribly mangled, his heel sticking out where his toes should have been.'

Sean McCann, Ballymena player, talking about the same game. When the RUC refused to help Jones, McCann came to his aid.

'I had just shaken hands with some of the Linfield players when someone hit me on the back of the head.'

Jimmy Jones, describing the start of the incident.

'Football in Northern Ireland has never been the same again, because as long as Celtic were in existence, our great players didn't have to move to England or Scotland to better themselves. There was no need.'

Jimmy Jones, on the fall-out of the 1948 game.

'Jones ran around like a deer with these others after him. This so called respectable man in a raincoat rushed forward and started kicking him. The police were standing around but they didn't do anything.'

Jimmy Kelly, journalist, reporting on the Jimmy Jones incident.

'The loss of Belfast Celtic was the blackest day in Northern Ireland football history, although maybe the way things have turned out over the past few years due to sectarianism, it may have been a good thing after all.'

Jimmy Jones.

'The Celtic players were treated like film stars so everyone wanted to play for the club, irrespective of religion. How good were we? We'd have finished in the top six in the English First Division, no bother.'

Jimmy Jones.

'Some of our team were too afraid to hit the ball.'

Harry Walker on the atmosphere in Windsor Park.

'When I saw uniformed policemen, who were supposed to be neutral, throwing their caps in the air with delight, I realised we were not going to have much protection at the end of the game.'

George Hazlett, on the Belfast Celtic v. Linfield game (1948).

'I can't stand on this spot and not see Celtic Park in my mind's eye. It's not a shopping mall to me, it's still Paradise, as everyone called it.'

Jimmy Jones.

'The only ground in Europe where the presence of the police would actually provoke a riot rather than prevent it.'

Eamonn McCann's description of the Derry City Ground, at Brandywell (1993).

'England can handle defeat very well, but they can't handle victory. It brings out the snarl factor.'

Colm Tóibín, writer (2002).

'I think going to football and fighting is an illness. I don't think you can stop.'

Chelsea-supporting hooligan interviewed by Donal MacIntyre (1999).

'Clegg is inno-cent, Clegg is inno-cent.'

English supporters chant at Ireland v. England (1995). Lee Clegg became a hero of the far right in England for shooting dead two Catholic teenagers in Belfast.

'Dublin away is always a big day out for those who are politically motivated. With the added antagonism of a ceasefire by the IRA being announced the previous week.'

Colin Ward, *All Quiet on the Hooligan Front: Eight Years That Shook Football* (1997). The match was played in February 1995, the ceasefire announced in August 1994.

'Ireland thinks it can beat the empire but we will kill as many Paddies as it takes.'

Supporters at Ireland v. England friendly match in February 1995. The match was abandoned when English fans rioted shortly after Ireland scored a goal.

'St George in my heart keep me English, St George in my heart I pray, St George in my heart keep me English, No Surrender, No surrender to the I-R-A.'

Chant by English supporters before they rioted at Ireland v. England (1995).

'We are a great nation, we win wars.'

English fans at Lansdowne Road (1995).

'When we get deported this is what we say, "We are England, we are England, God Save the Queen."'

Chant by English supporters before they rioted at Ireland v. England (1995).

'Somewhere in the twilight zone between sections UA and UB in the upper west stand of Lansdowne Road last night, Apocalypse England blew up again.'

Irish Press (16 February 1995).

'Somebody shouted, "Up the IRA." Nobody shouts at an English person and expects to get away with it.'

John from Nottingham, quoted in *Irish Press* (16 February 1995).

'The Italian fans bear most of the responsibility for the riot because they taunted the English fans by waving an Irish flag at them.'

World Soccer magazine, on a riot by English fans in Rome in October 1997. The Italian flag is green white and red.

'Society's values are such that one man's hooligan is another man's hero.'

Eamon Dunphy (1973).

Brian Kerr

Brian Kerr's wit was honed in Drimnagh and in the world of League of Ireland football, where pretensions and fools get short shrift. He was the Irish manager who gave the best pre-match and after-dinner talks, his diplomatic skills that would, they said, serve him well in the Middle East. How cruel that an offside goal in Tel Aviv finished his Irish managerial career.

'Winners are workers, losers use excuses.'
Slogan Brian Kerr had painted on the roof of the St Patrick's Athletic dressing room.

'I've been in positions at club level where you don't know whether the money is going to be there to pay the players and you're counting the crowd between corners and free-kicks. That's real pressure.'
Brian Kerr.

'The examinations come infrequently and are short. Those or 95 minutes control how everybody sees your work in the months surrounding the game, and even then you've no control because you're not out on the field. Still, it can be uniquely satisfying… When it goes well the buzz you feel for the few hours after a game is very special.'

Brian Kerr.

'There's one of those quotes that goes around in football, that there are only two things certain in life, death and the manager gets the sack, and I suppose I've just beaten one of them to the tape.'

Brian Kerr, on leaving St Patrick's Athletic to join the FAI.

'People measure a country by their football. Maybe not everyone, but people I know, when you say to them "Italy" they don't say "pasta", they say "football".'

Brian Kerr.

'Every preview of our games that I've read since setting down here, contained the sentence "it will be a battle of brain and brawn". And each time, I've tried to confront the journalist with the question of which team has the brawn?'

Brian Kerr, talking at the World Under-20 Championship in Malaysia.

'During Jack's time – and I don't want to underestimate the success he had – when I went to places and talked to people, outside all the "Olé Olé Olé" stuff after matches, they honestly didn't admire the way we played.'

Brian Kerr.

'If you want to know about the train timetables around England, then I'm your man.'

Brian Kerr on his battle to secure players for the under-16 and under-18 teams.

'We went out and played the Ajax system, three at the back, three in midfield, three up front, and a pair of rosary beads for Christy McEligott in goal.'

Brian Kerr, talking while manager at St Patrick's Athletic.

'To me, the football that Ireland teams played in the last ten years was Stone Age stuff. I'll admit that it was effective and brought us to a new level in the ratings. But anytime I went to international games at Lansdowne Road, it was, primarily, to watch the opposing team and how they set about handling Ireland's style.'

Brian Kerr (1996).

'It seems you can only play in the English Premiership these days if you are Italian and cost five million.'

Brian Kerr (1998).

'Football is fickle and people's opinions of football managers are fickle.'

Brian Kerr.

'Brian Kerr arrived, bubbling with enthusiasm and statistics. It might even have worked had he been able to make himself heard. But the Irish team were now lost in their own worlds behind the earphones of i-pods and as a nation we were locked into in the private bubbles of our grid-locked cars.'

Dermot Bolger.

'I'm sure all the experts – real or imagined – will have a field day.'

Brian Kerr, talking after his team failed to qualify for the 2006 World Cup finals.

'I'd say that was a Hail Mary pass.'

Brian Kerr.

'Of the 32 players who won the under-18 and under-16 championships for Ireland, 22 were from disadvantaged areas of Dublin. Nine of them were from Tallaght–Clondalkin. They wouldn't be great lads for going to school and they wouldn't be in the top four in Mensa but no better ambassadors for our country could you find.'

Brian Kerr.

'They are forever going on about psychology. My three Ps have nothing to do with psychology, they are passion, positive thinking and perseverance.'

Brian Kerr.

'You must be willing to do the work yourself, to create a good team attitude, is it really one for all and all for one, do we really tackle tasks together as a team.'

Brian Kerr.

'Football strategy is simple. Set a reasonable target and ask, "What do we need to do to reach it?" and work out what's stopping us from getting it.'

Brian Kerr.

'Everybody had to understand that an individualist like Robbie Keane had his part in the team. Liam George is the guy you'd bring to the Iraqi war, he'd be in the trenches fighting and then Robbie Keane would be coming out the door with the gun saying, "I got the general."'

Brian Kerr.

'You have got to emphasise the positive even when things are not going well. After losing 5–0 to England, I had to get all the management to tell them don't mention England. We beat Cyprus 5–1 and it was forgotten.'

Brian Kerr.

'When I was with Crumlin, teams like Home Farm would come in cars and we would come in runners with holes down the sides of them. In the dressing room, we would all do pull-ups and I would say, "Look at the other side, all their socks are down."'

Brian Kerr.

'The 21st was off-side.'

Brian Kerr, after his under-18 team beat a UN squad, Irish soldiers included, 22–0 in Cyprus.

'Passion on its own is nothing. In CYM, I would be giving my nice quiet team talk and you would hear the rugby team roaring and hanging their heads off the wall. Then they would charge on to the field and they were brutal.'

Brian Kerr.

'It is about balance: understanding the value in the team.'

Brian Kerr.

'Against England I gave them the holly, Cromwell, our mammies having to go to England to get work, all that. They went out with fire and passion and we were 3–0 down at half-time. At half-time, I gave a low-key talk and we only lost 5–0.'

Brian Kerr.

'He must have been back having a smoke with the goalkeeper.'

Brian Kerr.

'Extra time against Germany. If you thought you had extra time against Germany and the next goal was the winner, would you have said, "All right?" Think of it as a street game, when your ma is calling you in for dinner and you say next goal is the winner, and we play on for two and a half hours. And Alan Quinn said, "Yeah, right."'

Brian Kerr.

'It is not the big things that beat you it is the little things. There is an old Chinese proverb, "A man doesn't trip over a mountain, he trips over a stone."'

Brian Kerr.

'Bryan Robson's only words of wisdom were that the fourth penalty taker should always be good – to inspire confidence.'
Brian Kerr.

'Imagination is more important than power. Einstein said that, I was thinking of claiming it for myself.'
Brian Kerr.

'I was the one manager who went through nine chairmen. Most chairmen go through nine managers.'
Brian Kerr, after he left St Patrick's Athletic.

'An American basketball coach once said, "Those who are not fired by enthusiasm will be fired with enthusiasm."'
Brian Kerr.

'While I was manager of the Irish team, I had to put up with a series of letters, very vile and abusive letters, about the multiculturalism of the Irish team. I had Chris Hughton, a very Irish black man on the staff and I had black players on the team Clinton Morrison and Steven Reid. It was vile stuff, but it was sad really and it just shows you that there are some twisted minds around the place.'
Brian Kerr.

'When I pick a team I don't pick the eleven best, I pick the best eleven.'
Brian Kerr.

'Did he ever win a Hammond Cup in Division Two of the Leinster Senior League? I don't think so. What have I got to fear from Rainer Bonhoff.'

Brian Kerr, on his German counterpart, the 53-times capped Rainer Bonhoff.

Characters

Greater access into the personal lives of players means we get to know more about their eccentricities. The best stories are still reserved for late night discussions – which is just as well. Each passing generation mourns that there aren't any characters in the game anymore, but could it be that they are not looking closely enough?

'I asked for a Valderrama and I got a Val Doonican.'
Andy Townsend, on his new hairstyle for the 1994 World Cup finals.

'Roy arrived in the dining room just as we had started to eat and I was overcome by a sudden urge I should have controlled. Maybe it was a reaction to what had been written. Maybe, deep down, I was genuinely relieved to see him. I jumped up instinctively, bowed in homage and shouted, "Hallellujah." And he just looked at me with one of those world famous smirks that seemed to say, "Trigger, just shut your noise or I'll kick your f–king head in." So I did and just let him get on with it.'

Jason McAteer, from his 2002 World Cup diary.

'If you go into a shop and it's just Armani this and that, you buy it. Clothes that you don't even need. I spent a grand once. Bit of a waste really.'

Gary Kelly (1996).

'These days, I need a rub to get down the stairs in the morning.'

Niall Quinn (2002).

'The sending off? Well, Jason McAteer would annoy anyone.'

Roy Keane (2002).

'They called me Trigger at Sunderland because I once went into a pizza parlour and was asked whether I wanted it sliced into four or eight slices. I told them four because I couldn't manage eight slices.'

Jason McAteer.

'Jason McAteer's place is beside the hair dryer.'

Tour guide at Anfield.

'I thought about smashing everything in the room. I was really bitter and angry. The dummy wasn't going back in the pram.'

Jason McAteer, after being told he was dropped for the Germany game during the 2002 World Cup finals.

'Mark Kennedy reaches for the phone and orders breakfast in bed. He always has breakfast in bed and it always does my head in because we always get charged for it and I always end up with the bill.'

Jason McAteer.

'Ever since the revelation that Tony Cascarino dyed his hair close to contract negotiation time in order to maintain the illusion of youth, it has been impossible to look at older players without the gaze straying to their hairline.'

Jim White, journalist (December 2000).

'Zinedine Kilbane.'

Nickname for Kevin Kilbane.

'Following the recent freak storms in southeast England, many of London's finest trees have been destroyed or damaged. The condition of Niall Quinn was said to be satisfactory.'

When Saturday Comes (1988).

'I can't even remember when the seventies was.'

Robbie Keane.

'The managerial vacancy at the club remains vacant.'

Fran Fields.

'Then came the fifth penalty: Liam George as he walked up to take the penalty said he was thinking of his aunt in Coolock. And then he looked up at the goal. He imagined his da, who was from St Lucia, on one post saying put it here.

He imagined his ma on the other post, saying put it here. So he went for his ma because she is always right.'
Brian Kerr (1999).

'I should be the number one striker in Ireland, not number five.'
Telephone conversation with David Connolly, according to Don Givens.

'This makes Pat our top scorer.'
Jimmy Greaves, talking after Pat Jennings scored for Tottenham Hotspur with a long wind-assisted kickout during the Charity Shield match, the first match of the season, in 1967.

'Somewhere in there the grace of a ballet dancer joins with the strength of an SAS squaddie, the dignity of an ancient kind, the nerve of a bomb disposal officer.'
Eamon Dunphy, on the joys of goalkeeping.

'I am on this trip a much as a good-vibes man as a centre-forward. When things go bad, I am to burst into a chorus of "Always Look on the Bright Side of Life".'
Niall Quinn, *The Autobiography* (2002).

Commentary Box

Television audiences for Ireland's biggest soccer matches in the 1990s were among the highest for any sports fixture – 1.7 million for Ireland v. Norway in 1994, 1.5 million for Ireland v. England in 1990, 1.3 million for Ireland v. England in 1991. The penetration of soccer into people's lives was on a par with Uruguay, traditionally the most soccer-mad country per head of population in the world. People marked their lives by the great events and how they were described by commentators, who work to put words to the emotional intensity all around them. And there is a match going on as well. No wonder they make an occasional slip-up.

'The nation holds its breath.'
George Hamilton, speaking as Dave O'Leary prepared to take that penalty against Romania (1990).

'It's all over, he kept his head.'

George Hamilton, as Mendietta puts Ireland out of the 2002 World Cup finals.

'It's now 1–1, an exact reversal of the score on Saturday.'

Century Radio commentator.

'Thirty minutes to go, and it's still 1–0 apiece.'

Century Radio commentator.

'We'd be better off if it was 0–0 because we certainly don't want to get into the situation where we are protecting a 1–0 lead.'

Eoin Hand.

'Germany are probably, unarguably, undisputed champions of Europe.'

Bryan Hamilton.

'Mick McCarthy gave Ian Harte a special cuddle after he pulled him off.'

Barry Davies, BBC commentator.

'David O'Leary's poker face betrays the emotions.'

Clive Tyldesley.

'You'll see that many times but you won't see it all, it'll be called: What happened next.'

Darragh Maloney.

'The Spanish fans are encouraging their players to get forward and the Northern Ireland fans are also encouraging their players.'

Jackie Fullerton.

'The referee has sent the players to their eternal rest.'

Italian commentator.

'Tessem takes the free kick and Tessem heads it in at the far post.'

Stephen Alkin.

'Shelbourne are obviously having trouble with Bohemian's five-man back four.'

Eamonn Gregg.

'Paul Scholes with four players in front of him – five if you count Gary Neville.'

Darragh Maloney.

'Manchester United are looking to Frank Stapleton to pull some magic out of the fire.'

Jimmy Hill.

'The Stamford Bridge crowd is doing its own impersonation of silence.'

Stephen Alkin.

'Shay Given has shaken off a broken nose to play.'

Grandstand reporter.

'If he'd taken that it could have changed the whole complexity of the match.'
Ray Houghton.

'He'll be sent to Siberia.'
RTE commentator, remarking during an apocryphal Irish match against an eastern bloc country which allegedly brought a demand for an apology from the former Soviet Union.

'It's that sort of goal makes the hair stand on your shoulders.'
Niall Quinn.

'The Europeans just have to feel you and they will go down.'
Denis Irwin.

'He's gone too erect, no shape there, and there she goes.'
Noel King.

'We've got a moth in our commentary box, here's Vicente, Gerry has caught the moth just as Vicente was trying to sting like a butterfly, no, a bee of course.'
Jackie Fullerton.

'This is the last and final goal from the Turks.'
Damien Richardson.

George Hamilton

'By our calculations George is directly responsible for over 87 per cent of the goals the Irish national team have conceded.'
Larry Ryan, Gareth Power and Paul Little, authors of Dangerhere.com in the Gaffta Awards, 2005, noting George Hamilton's propensity to say something rash just before the opposition scores.

'The seeds of doubt that were sown at the weekend against Egypt have been doused by a dose of Jack Charlton's almighty weedkiller.'
George Hamilton, at Italia '90.

'It looks like the Mexicans have thrown their hat at it.'
George Hamilton

'There's no telling what the score will be if this one goes in.'
George Hamilton.

'Welcome to the Noucamp stadium in Barcelona, that is packed to capacity with some patches of seats left empty.'
George Hamilton.

'When I said they'd scored two goals, of course I meant they'd scored one.'
George Hamilton.

'The Baggio brothers, of course, are not related.'
George Hamilton.

'The eiderdown of this 2–0 lead is a lot more comfortable than the blanket of 1–0.'

George Hamilton.

'Here's Henry, trying to burst the bubble still further, if indeed it needs more bursting.'

George Hamilton.

'What that situation really needed was a little eyebrows.'

George Hamilton.

'The midfield are like a chef, trying to prise open a stubborn oyster to get at the fleshy meat inside.'

George Hamilton.

'We don't really know what Iran are capable of when the gun is put to their head.'

George Hamilton.

'Referee Norlinger is outstanding in the sense that he stands out.'

George Hamilton.

'It flew towards the roof of the net like a Wurlitzer.'

George Hamilton.

'Shay Given almost single-handedly won the match for Newcastle against Everton, although obviously he didn't score the goals.'

George Hamilton.

'He caught that with the outside of his instep.'
George Hamilton.

'And Hyppa rises like a giraffe to head the ball clear.'
George Hamilton.

'Glum Oranges. In fact I think the fruit their feelings are more akin to is a lemon.'
George Hamilton, after Ireland's win over Holland (2001).

'And Flavio Roma was left there like a jilted lover under Clery's clock.'
George Hamilton.

George Hamilton: 'Roy Carsley has it.'

Jim Beglin: 'Lee Carsley, George.'

George Hamilton: 'Ah yes, perhaps it's because his head reminds me of Ray Wilkins.'

'Real Madrid are like a rabbit in the glare of the headlights in the face of Manchester United's attacks. But this rabbit comes in the shape of a suit of armour in the shape of two precious away goals.'
George Hamilton.

'We're into the second minute of stoppage time of which there isn't one.'
George Hamilton.

Jimmy Magee

'Jean Tigana has spent the entire first half inside Liam Brady's shorts.'

Jimmy Magee.

'Apologies to our Costa Rican viewers for talking over their national anthem.'

Jimmy Magee, taking a leaf out of Micheál Ó Muircheartaigh's book.

'Ardiles strokes the ball like it was a part of his anatomy.'

Jimmy Magee.

'The reason for the delay to the kick-off is because it's not yet kick-off time.'

Jimmy Magee.

'Lee must attempt to keep Cech, the Czech, in check.'

Jimmy Magee.

'Fowler, living up to his name.'

Jimmy Magee.

'The man they call the monster.'

Jimmy Magee, introducing Horst Hrubesch at the end of the 1982 World Cup semi-final penalty shootout.

'Brennan blocking Blochin out of the game.'

Jimmy Magee.

'He's marking him so close he will probably go into the dressing room with him at half-time.'

Jimmy Magee.

'And on this occasion, Solis failed to find any light.'

Jimmy Magee.

'With the goal empty Nicky Butt, if he could manage it, should kick himself.'

Jimmy Magee.

'Sam Allardyce with the mobile phone and the chewing gum. Which will he swallow first?'

Jimmy Magee.

Tom Tyrrell

'We are about as far away from the penalty box as the penalty box is from us.'

Tom Tyrrell.

'The ball stuck to his foot like a magnet attracting a piece of steel, or metal rather.'

Tom Tyrrell.

'And there's a free kick now in the box, just in that little space between the eighteen-yard line and the six-yard line, that little incomplete rectangle, I don't know what you'd call it geometrically. That three-side rectangle.'

Tom Tyrrell.

'Stockdale is holding his head – I think he's hurt his leg.'

Tom Tyrrell.

'Veron's corner was a real inswinger, but it swung out before it swung in, if you get my drift.'

Tom Tyrrell.

'Most of the play is in the middle of the pitch, like a giant Easter egg.'

Tom Tyrrell.

'I don't think that was offside. You can see it on the big screen opposite but it's difficult to tell because your brain has to immediately reverse what you've just seen.'

Tom Tyrrell.

'Newcastle are finally going to end their London bogey. That would be a ghost – no, an albatross off their necks.'

Tom Tyrrell.

'There's an old saying in football that he who scores next when it's 3–1 can influence the outcome of a game.'

Tom Tyrrell.

'Giggs did everything there but either score or pass.'

Tom Tyrrell.

'They've got to retreat ten metres, or ten yards in old money.'

Tom Tyrrell.

'My eyes might have been deflected by Robbie Keane.'
Tom Tyrrell.

'When the game kicks off, it's over.'
Tom Tyrrell.

Conor MacNamara

'The trainers weren't on the pitch at all, and of course the referee doesn't have to take into consideration the minute's silence.'
Conor MacNamara.

'What United have unleashed at Old Trafford tonight they hope will take them all the way to the land of the trophy.'
Conor MacNamara.

'The longer the score stays at 0–0 the better for Barcelona, remember if they can score next week, it will be an away goal.'
Conor MacNamara.

'They say that football is unscripted drama and this match certainly hasn't followed the script tonight.'
Conor MacNamara.

Tommy Smyth

'Lebouef is so far up the field he will need to call a taxi to get back in time.'
Tommy Smyth.

'Venegoor just turns and lampoons it into the net.'
Tommy Smyth, ESPN's Irish commentator.

'I can't believe after 13 minutes of play that Zidane has perspired so much.'
Tommy Smyth, of ESPN, commenting on a Real Madrid v. Malaga match.

'There's Juan Carlos, the Spanish king, so there's royalty here besides ourselves.'
Tommy Smyth.

'Do you like your Hamburgers well done because they will be if they don't win today.'
Tommy Smyth, of ESPN, commentating on Hamburg SV.

'Liverpool don't do well in Italy, especially against Italian teams.'
Tommy Smyth.

Divorce:

Ireland's Two FAs

Soccer is the only sport with a major following on the island where Ireland fields two teams. How this came about is remarkably simple: a dispute over a replayed cup match. The fact that the country remained split has damaged the game on both parts of the island and some would argue, has prevented the growth of a strong and financially viable league. It was 1952 before the Irish League title was taken out of Belfast and 1933 before the League of Ireland title was taken out of Dublin. But despite occasional disputes, as in the early 1920s and early 1950s, cross-border contacts have remained consistently strong even in troubled times.

'No sporting code mirrored the political evolutions in Ireland of the 20th century more accurately than soccer or association football.'

Peter Byrne, *Official History of the FAI 75th Anniversary 1922-97*.

'"If others can do it, why can't we?" So often words along these lines can be heard when the chat comes round to the question of the All-Ireland Association Football team, the mythical team. The rugby people, the boxers, the hockey players to mention just a few from each side of the line dividing our country, get along like the proverbial house on fire. But why does this line also divide our football teams.'

Brendan McKenna, in the programme for a match between an All-Ireland soccer team and Brazil (1973).

'The FAI are a breakaway association and the junior partners. They would have to disband and reaffiliate to the senior body.'

Harry Cavan, President of the Belfast-based IFA (1973).

'We are two independent associations and neither would support unification. It would reduce the number of players who would gain international caps and would cut the number of clubs competing in European competitions.'

Jim Boyce, President of the Belfast-based IFA (1999).

'Realistically both football associations need a joint approach to the game. It must be possible to get rid of a lot of the meaningless competitions.'

Kevin Friel, chairman of Derry City.

'It is no reason to suppose that because Belfast is the cradle of Irish soccer it should be allowed to be its coffin.'

Old Bohemian letter to the *Evening Telegraph* (1920).

'The gates in the past six or eight weeks in Dublin have exceeded any previous year in the belief that the Dublin clubs are about to break with Belfast. The populace has come to the support of the game in numbers hitherto unequalled. The attachment of Belfast has always been viewed unfavourably by the bulk of the people in the game in Dublin and consequently has never enjoyed their support. Sunday soccer is taboo in Belfast in Dublin it is quite the reverse. A working understanding could be come to here between the Saturday and Sunday clubs. Soccer is rampant in France where it is quite common on Sunday. It is not outside the bounds of possibility to come to an understanding with the GAA. There is a great future in store for soccer and we in Dublin once we sever the ties with Belfast.'

Viator, *Sport* (28 May 1921).

'Any of the Dublin clubs who for a moment imagines that they are upholding the interest of the IFA by continuing their affiliation thereto are making a serious mistake and the quicker they take steps to sever the connection the better. Belfast doesn't want them and they are exposing themselves to the humiliation and contempt by continuing their attachment.'

Sport (12 March 1921).

'The hands of the clock have been put back two decades. There is not room for two associations and both the IFA and the Leinster body will soon find the new situation out.'

Jack McAlinden (28 May 1921).

'Football Unity At Last.'

Irish Independent (3 March 1932). Unfortunately the news was premature.

'The IFA to have permanent chairmanship of selection committee, and to keep all receipts from home internationals whether they be held in Dublin or Belfast.'

The IFA conditions that caused unity talks to break down in 1925 when agreement was close.

'The IFA to give one of two places on the international board to the FAI.'

The FAI condition that caused unity talks to break down in 1932 just when agreement seemed to have been secured.

"The idea of a reconciliation between the two Irish governing bodies has been dropped for the time being. The political situation instead of improving here has been growing worse daily and the outlook is bleak for every phase of life, sport included.'

Jack McAlinden (14 January 1922).

'We have our faults in Belfast, too many of them for the good of business and recreative enjoyment, but none can gainsay the fact that it was a great sporting city when the goods were served up. It is too soon to talk of a fusion of forces between the governing bodies but just as has occurred in the political world it has to come. There is no question. A divided Ireland in football won't tend to progress. There is room for one governing body and one only.'

Jack McAlinden (21 January 1922).

'We are all anxious to heal the dispute and the real men in both parties would settle it when the time arrives.'

Captain James Wilton, President of the Belfast-based IFA, at the IFA's AGM (1922).

'Headquarters in Dublin brings us to the political arena. This is where it will break down. Every single complaint can be ended if the question of a change in headquarters is dropped. The IFA will never consent to a change in headquarters. There the matter ends.'

Jack McAlinden (14 January 1922).

'Probably what weighed more than anything else is the fact that there are something like 600 clubs in the Free State whereas the IFA doesn't reach the 200 mark. Representation therefore on an All-Ireland Council would be two to one in favour of the South and everyone knows exactly what that means.'

Ralph the Rover, *Belfast Telegraph*. Negotiations on the 1932 solution broke down after nine days.

'Today we play under the title of Ireland. Since the inception of the Football Association of the Irish Free State, until our international last year, we have adopted the title of the Irish Free State in our endeavour to induce the Irish Football Association to play under the title of Northern Ireland. Both associations have had their areas of control defined as that of the Irish Free State and Northern Ireland respectively, and we have many times suggested that teams playing under the title of Ireland should by selected by an international committee, equally representative of both associations. So far this proposal has not been fully accepted by the Northern Association and the latter body has continued to play under the title of Ireland.'

Note in the programme for Ireland v. Germany (1936).

'Today we play for the first time under the new name conferred on us by the body that governs international football, the FIFA, and let us hope that under this new title, the Republic of Ireland we shall prove as successful as we did under our other names of the Irish Free State and Ireland.'

Note in the programme for Ireland v. Norway (1954).

'This is the best decision since Tom Farquarson of Cardiff City refused his cap when selected by the Northern Ireland FA in 1931. The position of the Northern Association could not long be maintained if other players acted as Martin did, and that the FAI would continue to struggle to get their international position right.'

Myles Murphy, FAI secretary.

'The Irish Football Association remains the national association, and indeed the only association entitled to use the title Ireland. Its territory may be reduced in size but in every other respect it remains unaltered. It carries the confidence of the other British associations and it takes its place in the British International Championship as Ireland and is the only body competent to do so. The Irish Football Association has suffered many attempts at interference with great tolerance but, in every instance they have acted within the laws and within their right and due regard to the rights of others. The Irish Football Association has been accepted and recognised as one of the four British associations since its formation seventy-four years ago, and is, in fact, the fourth oldest association in the world. All it asks is to be left alone to conduct its own business in its own country as the national association recognised by the other British associations and FIFA.'

Harry Cavan, IFA President, pleading to FIFA (1954).

'The Irish Football Association functioned harmoniously until a political movement caused re-adjustment of relations between Ireland and the British government. Prior to this international matches between Ireland and the other British Associations were arranged both in Dublin and in Belfast. The clubs whose headquarters were in the new Free State area and who were in full membership of the IFA seceded from the Association and formed a new Football Association for themselves. These clubs were at once suspended by the Irish Football Association, who desired to maintain the homogeneity of the Association, saw no reason why there should be two Football Associations in an area which hitherto had been happy with one. The point which is vital here is that it was the clubs in the new Free State who left the Irish Football Association and thus made themselves non-members. From time to time various suggestions were made and conferences held to formulate a working agreement between the two Associations. These conferences proved abortive, as they were bound to do with political influences as they existed in the Irish Free State. The title taken by the once Football Association of the Irish Free State should be altered to the real name of the country over which they claim jurisdiction – that is Éire. It is important to point out at this stage that association football is not recognised as their national game – which is called 'Gaelic' and is an amalgamation of association and rugby football. Although their territory may be greater than that of the Irish Football Association, there are vast tracts of the territory in which no association football is played at all.'

Harry Cavan, IFA president (1954).

'It makes no difference. We will continue to play as Ireland. They have been playing under that name for years anyway, only we have been doing it for fifty years longer.'

Fred Cochrane, President of the FAI.

'Unofficially some Southern Ireland [sic] legislating club men and even people outside football have recently approached players and asked them not to give their services to the North of Ireland, appealing to their patriotism.'

Ulster Newsletter (February 1948).

'I got a telephone call from the FAI asking me to refuse to play for Northern Ireland. I said I couldn't do it because it was too late. But on the same today that Ireland and Wales were playing, Aston Villa were playing Manchester United and Manchester Untied trounced Aston Villa. I arrived back at the Villa grounds and the chairman brought me up to his office and asked me, for Aston Villa's sake, to refuse to play for Northern Ireland. So I did it. I refused to play for Northern Ireland from then on and that was the end of the story.'

Con Martin.

'It was a magnificent gesture by a man who proved himself a great player and sportsman and must strengthen the position of the FAI in trying to achieve a united Ireland in the sport.'

J. J. Kane, FAI chairman, on Con Martin's 1948 policy of lobbying FAI players not to play for IFA teams.

Eamon Dunphy

Even if he had retired into obscurity when back problems brought his playing career to a premature halt, Eamon Dunphy's legacy would have been substantial. Capped 23 times for Ireland, he campaigned to get higher wages for soccer players in the English leagues, wore an armband in Millwall's match immediately after Bloody Sunday in 1973, stood for election for the English Labour Party, was one of the first Irish-born soccer players to get a coaching badge – and he wrote a memoir that changed the English soccer biography for ever. When he returned to join John Giles' new initiative at Shamrock Rovers, he set up a viable youth scheme which, like the Giles project, was about three decades ahead of its time.

But it is as a media figure rather than a footballer he will be remembered, as RTÉ's soccer panellist alongside Giles. He was given his first column in 1978 by *The Irish Times*, then moved through the *Sunday World* and *Sunday Tribune* to the *Sunday Independent*. Bullying, bombastic, entertaining and self-effacing in turn, he hounded Eoin Hand out of the Ireland job, attempted to do the same to Jack Charlton and Mick McCarthy, and managed to impose himself as a self-appointed gadfly in almost every debate concerning the changes in Irish society. The very name Dunphy is enough to start a debate on its own. So here goes.

'The first two-syllable word I ever learned growing up was discretion.'

Eamon Dunphy.

'I have discovered the hard way that for a vocal majority the World Cup is not about sport after all.'

Eamon Dunphy, during the 2002 World Cup, *Ireland on Sunday*.

'The image of the professional footballer as a glamorous showbusiness type, surrounded by pretty girls and flash cars, is firmly implanted in most people's minds. I know him more accurately as the deeply insecure family man or the tearful failed apprentice.'

Eamon Dunphy, *Only a Game* (1976).

'I don't like amateurs. They get up my nose. I know football as my living, as a hard life, my wife and child's livelihood. Football is a joy to them, plus a tenner in the boot as a bonus. And you can be the local hero in Hitchin or Wycombe. It's nice. No pressure. You have got your job and your family; so you can ponce around every Saturday, do a little bit, and you are a star. Amateurs' lives are a bit luxurious.'

Eamon Dunphy, *Only a Game* (1976).

'A flowerpot.'

Eamon Dunphy, describing of Ray Treacy during the 1984 European Championship.

'Michel Platini has no bottle. He is not a great player.'

Eamon Dunphy, spawning a thousand parodies during the 1984 European Championship.

'The Great War? It was a good war, not a great war.'

Gary Cooke, Dunphy satirist, on RTÉ's *Scrap Saturday*.

'Keep them coming, we'll need them for the libel case.'

Eamon Dunphy, appealing for more messages from supporters to his radio show during the 2002 World Cup finals.

'A failed Third Division footballer,'

Description of Eamon Dunphy in letter to *Sunday Tribune* (1982).

'I will have you know that I am not a failed Third Division footballer, I am a failed Second Division footballer.'

Eamon Dunphy's response.

'If ever a player was out of his class that night it was me. The pace of the game was far greater than I had ever experienced. The skill of the opposition was unbelievable. Even my own colleagues from first and second division clubs, were geared to a far faster game than I anticipated.'

Eamon Dunphy, on his international debut, a play-off between Ireland and Spain for the 1966 World Cup finals.

'Eamon was reading those strange books. He seemed to get into some very intellectual books.'

Joe Kinnear, on sharing a room with Dunphy on Irish team trips, quoted in Paul Rowan, *The Team That Jack Built* (1994).

'Call me a traitor, but I can't cheer for Ireland now.'

Eamon Dunphy, writing about the 2002 World Cup finals, *Ireland on Sunday*.

'Dunphy's criticism wasn't constructive. It was destructive. He got the knife into Eoin. That was the downfall of Eoin Hand. If he hadn't lived in Ireland, the pressure wouldn't have got to him. And the pressure did get to him in the last year.'

Terry Conroy, quoted in Paul Rowan, *The Team That Jack Built* (1994).

'No football team will win this tournament. This tournament will be won by the faceless empires of corporate greed. The Jules Rimet trophy has become hijacked by the world of big business b—ds, sold to the TV networks of Satan. There will be a final on July 12th. It will have no soul. It will be between Nike and Snickers.'

Gary Cooke, imitating Eamon Dunphy, *Après Match* (2002).

'Eamon Dunphy is a nobody with one virtue, honesty and realism.'

Dunphy, paying tribute to himself.

'I created a monster. The Mary Shelley of Irish journalism, that's me.'

Seamus Martin, who encouraged Dunphy's controversial style as his sport editor at the *Sunday Tribune* 1980–82.

Dunphy and Charlton

Jack Charlton had been warned that Dunphy had hounded Eoin Hand out of the Ireland job. Dunphy's mission to destroy Jack was menacing but in the end unsuccessful. His criticism of Charlton's style of football has given him an enduring cameo role in the history of Irish soccer during the Charlton years.

'I'm bigger than you.'
Jack Charlton, talking at his first press conference in charge of the Irish team.

'I'm never going to please everybody. Everybody's not a purist. People don't have to agree with the way we play. Dunphy eventually will have his day because things will go wrong for us at some stage. But I'll fight that as long as I can.'
Jack Charlton (1991).

'What Dunphy wrote about Mick McCarthy after coming back from the European Championship was a disgrace, for someone who had given as much as Mick had given. I decided I wouldn't do anything with Dunphy ever again.'

Jack Charlton (1991).

'Football's answer to Andy Capp.'

Eamon Dunphy, on Jack Charlton.

'I'm not a thick, ignorant Andy Capp Geordie, I won't answer to that. I do a professional job, and I know the game of football. I'll discuss it and I'll argue it with anyone. I was asked to do a job for the Irish and I did it in a way that I felt needed to be done.'

Jack Charlton (1991).

'My refusal to answers questions from Dunphy was the biggest mistake I ever made. I made Eamon very, very famous. It's a talking point to this day. I have never got involved with him from that day to this.'

Jack Charlton.

'All of a sudden we got to the World Cup and he annoyed us before the start because we were supposed to go and train in the stadium, and him and his pal stood right in the middle of the gateway. As soon as the players got off the bus the first people we could see were them. Then came the press conference, and I made a mistake: I said I didn't want to talk to him. What I should have done is ignored him completely which I'd done for two years and I've done since and gone to

some other question. But I didn't. I made him even more famous than he was.'
Jack Charlton (1991).

'I know you. You are a trouble maker.'
Jack Charlton, talking to Dunphy at his first press conference as Ireland manager.

'Give him a lash Jack.'
T-shirt depicting Charlton kicking Dunphy, sold after Dunphy's 'Egypt' outburst (1990).

Euro '88

Ireland had played well in the qualifiers for the 1988 European Championship, beating Scotland in Hampden to bring an inglorious away record to an end. But defeat in Sofia seemed to scupper their chances. The manner of Ireland's qualification for the finals became an important part of the folklore, with Gary Mackay's unlikely late goal for Scotland against Bulgaria putting Ireland in the tournament. Ireland were deprived of a place in the semi-finals by an offside goal and the recriminations over tactics gave us a hint of what was to come. In the manner of these things, the event was accorded greater importance than it probably deserved as a turning point in Irish popular culture, a stepping-off point in Irish society or a kick-off point for the economic boom that another economist would turn into a cliché all its own – the 'Celtic Tiger.'

'Who put the ball in the England net? I did.'
Ray Houghton, talking at the homecoming in Dublin.

'England Stuttgart June 12. The game we won and should have lost. Soviet Union, Hanover June 15. The game we drew and should have won, and Holland, Gelsenkirchen, June 18, the game we lost and should have drawn.'

The summary of Euro '88 in Sean Ryan, *The Boys in Green* (1997).

'Forget the penalty save. England in Stuttgart was my best performance of all. As a sports person when you give the nation something they can remember no matter what you do after. That will always remain with them. To give something that people hang on to. You give them that you will be a hero forever after.

Packie Bonner.

'On terraces in Stuttgart, Hanover and Gelsenkirchen, the notion of Jack's Army was invented. People returned from Germany with stories to tell and a new national obsession began.'

Dermot Bolger.

'We got to Gelsenkirchen, made it to the stadium down that avenue of stones, got past the Dutch in a mass of orange on three sides and packed into one corner of the crowd behind Packie Bonner's goal. There were faces we knew from Hanover and Stuttgart, faces from Dublin, faces we'd never known before, piled in one solid mass of green. And when it began, we screamed and we shouted and sang our hearts out for the lads. For Packie Bonner, for Tony Galvin running himself into the ground, for Frankie Stapleton suddenly old and making us old, holding up the ball, snatching those few extra seconds that crawled by. Paul McGrath rose at the far post and we rose with him.'

Dermot Bolger, *In High Germany*, a play set during the 1988 European Championship finals (1990).

'I knew things had changed when my coalman started talking about Gelsenkirchen. "Gelsen-kirchen." How he loved to pronounce the word.'

Nell McCafferty.

'We had to let the fans in. None of us knew how to play the fiddle.'

Paul McGrath, explaining why supporters were allowed to join the team celebrations after the victory over England.

'I have Gary Lineker's shirt up in my room and it has only stopped moving now.'

Mick McCarthy.

'We got away with a lot of things out there.'

Jack Charlton.

'England have not so much been executed by the Irish as found guilty of committing suicide by missing so many goal chances.'

Daily Mail, on Ireland v. England.

'England were beaten by a bunch of boyos from their own backyard.'

The Sun.

'Something-ov, I think.'

Ronnie Whelan, asked whose jersey he had swapped after the match against the Soviet Union.

'More people know where Ireland is today than ever before.'

Jack Charlton after Euro '88.

'We were perceived to be the pub team of the tournament, a happy-go-lucky bunch who partied with their supporters and were just happy to be involved. We had a good card school going and at the end of the tournament a lot of money had been won and lost.'

Tony Cascarino, *Full Time: The Secret Life of Tony Cascarino* (2000).

George Hamilton: 'Well Jack, the impossible dream is over.'

Jack Charlton: 'What do you mean, impossible. We went within seven minutes of getting into the semi-finals. What's impossible about that?'

'I've seen it in Walt Disney's *Sleeping Beauty*, the castle waking from centuries of sleep. Nobody shouts in the Cross Guns. Not at first. There is no euphoria. There is shock. People look at the screen, then at their glasses, then at each other. They look back at the screen. Injury-time is approaching. We're on the verge of qualifying for something and we aren't even playing.'

Dermot Bolger, describing how Gary Mackay's goal put Ireland into the European Championship.

'We had it all mapped out, our team would be built around David O'Leary, Mark Lawrenson, Frank Stapleton and Liam

Brady. And when we crossed the Red Sea, only Frank, the eternal survivor, was on board. Injury had guillotined Mark's career, Liam was in the repair shop, David was the victim of selectorial myopia. And young lads who were hardly a wet season in football partook of the glory in West Germany.'

Con Houlihan.

'John you haven't scored for Ireland yet so don't go breaking the bait of a lifetime this afternoon.'

Jack Charlton, talking to John Aldridge on the morning of Ireland v. England.

'The funny thing is I didn't score that many goals in my career. I had never scored for Ireland before Stuttgart. And that goal was just a matter of being in the right place at the right time. I think anyone in that position would have been expected to score.'

Ray Houghton.

'I feinted to make a run and come back inside. The ball just appeared. Mick had thrown it 40 yards and it came out of the sky nicely, I thought, Why not? People can only laugh at you if you fall over and miss it. I didn't even catch it right. It more or less caught on the top of my foot and the bottom of my shin. It looped into the top corner.'

Ronnie Whelan, on his goal against the Soviet Union in Hanover.

'I've got a fishing trip booked for next weekend and I don't want to be stuck in Germany for a bloody European Championship final.'

Jack Charlton, during Euro '88.

FAI, Oh Sweet FA-Eye:
The Football Association of Ireland

Chosen by the divines to run Irish soccer since 1922, they have sometimes been slightly overwhelmed by the task. But how we love them.

'I've got the perfect relationship with these guys, they love me and I hate them.'

Liam Tuohy, Ireland manager on his relationship with Merrion Square officialdom (1972).

'From information I have picked up on my travels, I would say that England, Ireland (North and South), Wales and Scotland are the only countries in which the international teams are chosen by men lacking an obvious footballing background. Surely that cannot be a good thing.'

Tom Finney, England player, speaking in the 1950s.

'I'll get you on the Irish team if you sign for Drums.'

Sam Prole, FAI Chairman, to Donal Leahy of Cork.

'The train was overbooked and the players ended up in the luggage compartment for three hours while the officials were in the regular compartment.'

Joe Kinnear, talking about a journey between Poznan and Berlin (1970).

'In general, there is not a culture of discipline in the management of the FAI, with most basic management disciplines non-existent.'

The Genesis Report.

'Irish football story goes back seventy years and it's a tread that incompetence and stupid administration has robbed Irish football. There is a poverty of aspiration and poverty of expectation. I want a bleeding revolution.'

Eamon Dunphy.

'We've been dealing with some dishonourable people over the course of this whole affair and I'm not talking about the FAI.'

Pat Devlin, Bray Wanderers manager, on his club's dispute with Bohemians over the suspension of striker Jason Byrne for an FAI Cup semi-final at Dalymount Park (2001).

'I'm sure Ireland and Germany will get on like a house on fire.'

FAI official, after Ireland's match with Germany in a still bombed-out Hamburg (1955).

'Too many fellows in the FAI still have their bicycles chained to the railings in Merrion Square.'

Billy Morton, when asked if he would become Secretary General of the FAI (1968).

'What do you mean it wasn't a good trip. Not at all. The hotels were excellent, the food was great. There was nothing disastrous about the tour.'

FAI official, after Ireland returned from their disastrous South American tour of 1982. During the tour, they were beaten 1-0 by Chile, 7-0 by Brazil (a record for the FAI) and 2-1 by Trinidad and Tobago.

'Some of the Irish players were travelling under British passports and were in fear they would be arrested at Buenos Aires airport.'

David O'Leary.

'Certain allegations have been made about me and I know who the alligators are.'

Peadar O'Driscoll, FAI Secretary General (attrib.).

'By the way, any chance of a ticket.'

Eoin Hand, Ireland manager, finishing his good luck call to the England manager Ron Greenwood before the 1982 World Cup finals. The FAI didn't get Hand accredited.

'I went into training the following day wearing the Poland shirt to wind up the English lads.'

Joe Kinnear, after Ireland's 1-0 win over Poland in 1973. Poland had just put England out of the World Cup.

'RTÉ are monopolists.'

Brendan Menton, FAI Chief Executive, on the Sky deal (July 2002).

'It's a funny old organisation.'

Brendan Menton, FAI Chief Executive, echoing Jimmy Greaves' assessment of soccer.

'The dictionaries were out that night.'

Donie Forde, recalling an FAI meeting to decide the eligibility of Raich Carter (1953).

'The honour of playing for your country if you are a professional footballer is directly related to the honour that's inherent in the organisation.'

Eamon Dunphy, quoted in Paul Rowan, *The Team That Jack Built* (1994).

'No sooner had players been nominated for the green jersey than an epidemic of injuries broke out or clubs flatly refused to release the chosen.'

Noel Dunne, *Bass Book of Irish Soccer* (1974).

'Although I was picked for a lot of games I only played in half of them. Often I had injuries but on other occasions Manchester Untied, through Matt Busby, influenced me not to play, and saw to it that I didn't lose out on the match fee.'

Tony Dunne.

'The shirt we used to play in was more like a rugby jersey. As for the shorts, I don't know who they ever thought played for

Ireland. They would put Johnny Giles and Joe Haverty into size 44 shorts. In the dressing room sometimes they'd pull the shorts over their heads. Occasionally you'd see Giles with a rolled-up pair of shorts and it tucked in like a great, baggy thing. Joe Haverty was a tiny little man and it was the funniest thing to see Joe in an Irish strip. Fellows like myself would bring our own shorts. Charlie Hurley would bring his own shorts too. We wouldn't accept it.'

Noel Cantwell, quoted in Colm Keane, *Ireland's Soccer Top Twenty* (2004).

'Joe Wickham used to phone you or you got a letter up to say you were selected. The itinerary would tell you to bring your own soap, your own towel, your own everything. You would report at a certain time and that was it.'

Noel Cantwell, quoted in Colm Keane, *Ireland's Soccer Top Twenty* (2004).

'You'd finish at five o'clock on a Saturday. And then get a police escort to the station, and then to the airport. It was sometimes impossible to get the plane so you'd have to get the boat, a journey of ten hours to Liverpool. I came over for the ferry for the game against Spain in 1965.'

Charlie Hurley, quoted in Paul Rowan, *The Team That Jack Built* (1994).

'They couldn't afford the flights in those days and so we'd go on the boat on the Saturday night after playing for our clubs and if the crossing was bad we wouldn't get much sleep. Then we'd check in to the Four Courts Hotel, which was where we stayed. We had three or four hours sleep and then we'd go down with our boots and everything else to the Gresham Hotel and assemble there at 12 o'clock.'

Noel Cantwell, quoted in Colm Keane, *Ireland's Soccer Top Twenty* (2004).

'The amount of times you'd turn up with six players missing and see two or three players from the League of Ireland who didn't know anything about international football, absolutely in awe of it all.'

Charlie Hurley, quoted in Paul Rowan, *The Team That Jack Built* (1994).

'We started out in international football fifty years ago. But I would say that without doubt we have not made the slightest progress in that time, on or off the field.'

Patsy McGowan, kicking off the FAI's 50th anniversary celebrations in 1971, quoted in Paul Rowan, *The Team That Jack Built* (1994).

'I got 43 caps for Ireland and about 40 of them were against Poland. Myself and Tomaszewski were like blood brothers, and most of the players knew each other by their first names. We'd kick in down the same end before the game.'

Ray Treacy, quoted in Paul Rowan, *The Team That Jack Built* (1994).

'We were always in Poland and we couldn't figure out why we were always in Poland. But one of the committee member's friends had a business in Poland. So I have more Polish caps than any other kind. Czechoslovakia was another favourite team for us. We were always behind the Iron

Curtain. We became the local team after a few years we were over there so often.'

Alan Kelly, quoted by Colm Keane, *Ireland's Soccer Top Twenty* (2004).

'It wasn't the manager's fault. It wasn't the hotel's fault. It was the fault of someone in a five star hotel 200 miles away.'

Mark Lawrenson, commenting on conditions in Bygodzcz during a 1981 trip to Poland, quoted in Paul Rowan, *The Team That Jack Built* (1994).

'Soccer was a fourth, fifth or tenth rated sport in Ireland. There was hurling, Gaelic football, the horse, the dogs and I should imagine darts and dominoes.'

Mick McCarthy, commenting on soccer's status in Ireland prior to Jack Charlton.

'In respect of present from Spain, a bottle of wine to be given to each player who travelled to Czechoslovakia and the balance left to be partaken at the last council meeting.'

FAI decision after Ireland's win in Prague in 1967 put Spain into the quarter-finals of the European Championship. According to Charlie Hurley he never got his bottle, quoted in Paul Rowan, *The Team That Jack Built* (1994).

FAI selector: 'That was the best performance from an Irish side in years.'

Johnny Giles: 'But we were wearing our away strip.'

Johnny Giles apocryphal story of international in which Ireland were beaten 4–0.

'Sure I had never heard of FIFA in those days.'

Kevin O'Flanagan, on the lack of preparation for the 1938 World Cup qualifier against Norway. The players were unaware it was a World Cup qualifier.

Sonny Molloy: 'Me go, get taxi, bring taxi.'

Paddy Bradshaw: 'Who do you think I am, a f–king Indian.'

Exchange between Irish players after match against Hungary, there no interpreters so players were in the habit of speaking pidgin English when they were abroad (1938).

'You'd have some real potato pickers coming out to play. A selector with a bit of clout would want to pick some of his boys. You have a League of Ireland player capped and right away he's worth a few thousand quid.'

Charlie Hurley, quoted in Paul Rowan, *The Team That Jack Built* (1994).

'In Bremen our flags were flown though, of course, well out-numbered by the swastika. We also, as a compliment, gave the German salute to their anthem, standing to attention for our own. We were informed this would be appreciated by their public which it undoubtedly was. The German Sports Minister at the Banquet paid special tribute to our playing the match as arranged despite what he described as untrue press reports regarding the position in Germany and their intentions.'

Official Report of FAI by Joe Wickham (1939), quoted in Sean Ryan, *The Boys in Green* (1997).

'I had brought a party of English journalists to Tempelogue tennis club the night before and hadn't got home until nearly two in the morning. I had a pub in town and was working from ten in the morning. Around ten to two, I got a phone call from Tommy Hutchinson, the Bohemian member of the selection committee, telling me I was playing against England at Dalymount at 2.30.'

Mick O'Flanagan, on his surprise selection for Ireland against England (1946).

'Secretary to arrange for information from English clubs regarding players playing the previous day immediately by phone after their matches on the Saturday and the Committee to meet if necessary on Saturday evening.'

Minutes of FAI selection committee (1948).

'A pattern was emerging after the war. With more Irish players based in England and Scotland playing full-time football, the part time League of Ireland player, who had been a mainstay before the war, was being phased out. The team should have been stronger for that, but the results were, if anything, poorer. Something was wrong with the set-up, but it would take many years of hard lessons before the correct answer would be forthcoming.'

Sean Ryan, *The Boys in Green* (1997).

'We used to turn up at the Gresham Hotel at 12 on Sunday not knowing who would arrive over from England. League of Ireland players would then be called in if there were any vacancies.'

Paddy Coad, capped eleven times for Ireland 1946–52.

'I voted for Eoin Hand because I think Paddy Mulligan was the one who threw a bun at me on one of my foreign trips.'
FAI official, after Eoin Hand had beaten Mulligan to the position of Ireland manager on a vote of 9-7.

'They are running it like a Mickey Mouse club. They can have the others but they can't have you.'
Matt Busby, after Tony Dunne returned from and Irish match with an injury.

'Just when English clubs decided to take the game of football seriously as a business, their Irish equivalents went about destroying the brand that had a willing loyal consumer base of close to 100,000 in Dublin alone.'
David McWilliams, economist.

'Had he signed the cheques?'
Member of Irish team after hearing that FAI secretary Joe Wickham had died during match in Katowice.

'A constantly exploding clown's car.'
Michael Nugent, one of the authors of *I Keano*, describing the public perception of the FAI.

'After Genesis, it's time for Exodus.'
Gerry McDermott, *Irish Independent*.

Famous Last Words

Ah yes, how we love to tempt fate. The vote of confidence form the chairman of the board is enough to send fear down the spine of any soccer manager. The vows of lasting friendship that are meant to disguise the fact it will all end in tears. And the long odds that seduce even bookmakers into a false sense of security. Ireland were 11–1 to beat England at Goodison in 1949 and 8–1 in Stuttgart in 1988.

'With Keane to lead us there, there's nothing to fear/Because this time 2002 is going to be our year.'
Ireland's official song for the 2002 World Cup finals. It remained unchanged.

'As Mick McCarthy and the chosen few selected to carry the dreams of the nation, flew out from Dublin Airport, that revered Doctor of Laws and sometime footballer Roy Keane was asked what did he make of the election, "I have more important things to worry about," he answered. And all at once, we knew our dreams were in safe hands.'

Irish Independent (18 May 2002).

'I think I've only had a couple of bookings in the last few games, which is good for me. I better not say any more about that or I'll probably get sent off tonight.'

Roy Keane, quoted in the *Evening Herald*, before he got sent off against Russia (1996).

'Céad Míle Fáilte from the six counties.'

Banner at Ireland v. England match (1995). The match was abandoned when England fans rioted.

'There will be no repeat of the problems experienced by the players involved in World Cup '94 in Orlando.'

Mick McCarthy, *Ireland on Sunday* (March 2002).

'Anyone who thinks that Éire will defeat England at Goodison this afternoon, southern Irishmen excluded, needs to have his brains tested.'

Henry Rose of the *Daily Express*, later to perish in the Munich air crash, before Ireland v. England in Goodison Park (1949).

'If Manchester United are beaten I will present my show in the nude.'

Eamon Dunphy. He did.

'Previously we used to fly into Dublin for a match and fly out afterwards. Some of the players didn't even know each other. And there was a big difference in class between the professional players in the English League and the home-based players. Johnny Giles has made all the difference in the world. Under such a good manager we can win the championship.'

Joe Kinnear, predicting that Ireland would win the 1976 European Championship.

'Ireland are no-hopers, they are ranked eighth out of eight teams in the tournament.'

Bobby Robson, England manager, before England lost their opening match of Euro '88 to Ireland.

'The Irish were always going to be a difficult proposition. We should have won, we had 18 chances to their one. I felt if we had got one goal we could have got two or three.'

Bobby Robson, twenty-four hours later.

'If Shelbourne win the cup, I'll eat my hat.'

Gerry Noone, the 'Whistler,' *Evening Press* soccer correspondent and later sports editor of *The Irish Times*. He was photographed eating his hat after Shels won the cup in 1960.

'Czechoslovakia 10 Ireland 0.'

Sign held up by fans before Ireland's 2–1 shock win in Prague in the final qualifier for the 1968 European Championship.

'On the field he is a major asset. Off it he's quite unassuming. An ordinary lad. He'll say, "What are you all doing tonight?" And he'll come to the pictures or whatever. What you see on the pitch is an unusually extravagant character but he's not like that off it.'

Mick McCarthy, talking about Roy Keane before the 2002 World Cup.

'Roy Keane could replace Brian Kerr as Ireland manager if they fail to qualify for the World Cup.'

The Guardian.

'Roy Keane is set to rebuff approaches to make him the manager of the Republic of Ireland if Brian Kerr is sacked next week.'

The Independent.

'Poland have to score twice now to draw and they will not do that.'

George Hamilton, tempting fate when Ireland were 3–1 up during a qualifier for Euro 1992 in Poznan.

'I might be tempting fate but I can't see the Poles scoring, oh NOOOOO, I just have.'

George Hamilton, seeing Ireland's qualification come undone in the same match.

'And Bonner has gone 165 minutes of these championships without conceding a goal. Oh danger here…'

George Hamilton.

'Shamrock Rovers will be capable of winning the European Cup in seven years.'

John Giles, speaking on his return to Irish soccer (1977).

'I've no nerves going to Wembley.'

Alan Kelly, goalkeeper, before playing England at Wembley in 1957. England beat Ireland 5-1. He paid at the turnstiles to watch the return match at Dalymount.

'A plush holiday home in Ireland and membership of the local golf club point the way to Johnny Giles' future.'

News of the World (1976).

'With many people not exactly ecstatic with the present squad containing too many English-born players, imagine the outcry if an Englishman became manager.'

Letter to *Supporters News* just before Jack Charlton was appointed manager of the Irish team.

'Leadership, a sense of purpose has been restored to the Irish team. Decentskinmanship has finally been dispensed with.'

Eamon Dunphy, hailing Jack Charlton as the new manager of the Irish team (1986).

'I don't want to tempt fate, but Thierry Henry is not having one of his best nights.'

Jim Beglin, RTÉ co-commentator, minutes before guess what?

'If ever a picture told a thousand words, the embrace of Mick McCarthy and Roy Keane after the final whistle in

Lisbon on Saturday night exploded the myth that the two men are at war.'

Philip Quinn, *Irish Independent* (2001).

'Roy Keane would never let his emotions destabilise the team.'

Niall Quinn.

Fans

The legend started with two railway workers, Paddy Synnott and Paddy Lawler, who travelled on an odyssey through war-torn Germany and Austria in May 1952, on the boat train from Holyhead to London, on to Dover, Ostend, Cologne, a 2 a.m. train through Nuremburg, Linz, across the Danube through the bureaucracy of the Russian occupation forces and on to Vienna to see Ireland lose 6–0.

In 1957, a record 3,000 supported Ireland in their World Cup qualifier against England in Wembley. And after the 1970s, there was, if not a travelling army, a travelling battalion of supporters, up to 12,000 of them for big events like the 1990 World Cup quarter-final in Rome, the 1997 World Cup play-off in Brussels and the 2004 World Cup qualifier in Paris. They gained a reputation for keeping their spirits up through defeat and keeping their heads as they were sneered at, taunted and abused – and that's just by Eamon Dunphy.

'Irish soccer fans are what this is all about. They deserve the best. They deserve the truth.'
Eamon Dunphy, World Cup panellist (2002).

'Flag-waving leprechauns.'
Eamon Dunphy, describing Irish fans at the World Cup (2002).

'The most arrogant, most optimistic country in the world.'
Gerry Ryan, broadcaster, describing Irish fans at the World Cup (2002).

'It was another of those days for the rest of the football world to watch and wonder. At how so many Irish fans could travel so far and celebrate so enthusiastically when once again their team had only earned a draw.'
Emmet Malone, journalist, during 2002 World Cup finals
The Irish Times.

'Seven Irish geezers go to Rec-the-Kip, Iceland, 300 years.'
Irish fans who saw Ireland win their first silverware in Iceland (1986).

'They've charged me with causing a breach of the peace for no apparent reason. We've just beaten Italy 1–0 and they call that for no apparent reason.'
Brian Byrne, an actor in Manhattan, charged with invading the field after the Italian match (1990).

'At a funeral in Wicklow, the coffin was brought out of the church just as Dave O'Leary scored his famous penalty against Romania. The priest said Amen to a stunned reaction. Then the mourning relatives burst into a dance of joy to the utter amazement of a passing American tourist.'

Anecdote in *What's the Story?*, compiled by Derek O'Kelly and Shay Blair (1992).

'Davy Keogh Says Goodbye.'

Friend of Davy Keogh, after he legged it with his 'Davy Keogh Says Hello' banner following an incident with a can of tar and a hotel room carpet (1992).

'Demented Chickens of Tramore.'

Supporters' banner, early 1990s.

'Ashbourne says howya.'

Supporters' banner, early 1990s.

'Win or lose we're for the booze.'

Fan's T-shirt, early 1990s.

'FIFA told the FAI at one point that the flags with the names of pubs on them would have to come down as they constituted advertising for outlets which encouraged people to drink alcoholic products other than that of main sponsors, Budweiser. On this one, the FAI held firm. And FIFA were thus spared a riot.'

Miriam Lord, *Irish Independent*, reporting from World Cup finals (2002).

'The growing injury list for spectators at home (twisting their ankles, jabbing themselves in the eye with glass tumblers or fainting with excitement) seems likely to make Mick McCarthy's injury worries pale into insignificance.'

Dr L. C. Luke, consultant at Cork University hospital, during the 2002 World Cup finals.

'The people of Ireland have been behaving while the English have not been behaving. They sang and they enjoyed it and they never caused a moment's problem.'

Jack Charlton.

'Baah, baah, baah.'

Irish supporters' reaction to being corralled in a cage at the docks in Sicily during Italia '90.

'Our husbands think we are shopping in Dublin.'

Supporters' banner, Portugal (1995).

'More than 65,000 piled into the same stadium that will stage the World Cup final on June 30. To the naked eye, at least 80 per cent of those gathered were wearing green. What conclusions to draw? Perhaps there are cows swaying in the fields at home, bloated and un-milked. Perhaps factories are silent and accumulating dust. Or perhaps, it is just that the great Irish Diaspora has responded to a flaringly honest team.'

Vincent Hogan, *Irish Independent*, 2002 World Cup finals.

'What will you say to the "Olé-Olérs" with the plastic hammers who worship you and are fascinated with your self-perpetuating egotism?'

Après Match parody of the 2002 Keane saga.

'Jack Charlton's sides never claimed to be entertainers. The style was rugged, formidably energetic, but ugly. All the exuberance was left to the fans.'

Fintan O'Toole (2001).

'That's the amazing thing about the Irish fans. They are the only supporters at this World Cup who will tell you – and mean it – that it's not actually winning that counts, it's playing the game with a bit of an attitude.'

Joseph O'Connor, in his World Cup diary, *The Secret World of the Irish Male* (1994).

'I hope you get the players going a bit faster than those moving statues.'

Fan, to Jack Charlton after his appointment as Irish team manager in 1986, quoted in Paul Rowan, *The Team That Jack Built* (1994).

'Championez Championez, olé olé olé.'

Northern Ireland fans after the team had gone through a world record 1,299 minutes in more than 13 matches without scoring a goal in international football, against Norway in February 2004.

'I do not know if you have ever spent much time in the company of Irish men who are far away from home, in a hot climate, with only a large group of stuffed animals for company, but if you haven't take my advice. Don't.'

Joseph O'Connor, in his World Cup diary, *The Secret World of the Irish Male* (1994).

'She said, "Er, some of the rides have been here for a long time, but other rides are new, and here at Disney we are constantly looking at ways to make rides more exciting." The fans are slapping their thighs and guffawing at this stage. One usually quiet man from Laois is actually honking with laughter.'

Joseph O'Connor, describing Disneyland Orlando ('the name of a city and not the name of an Irish soccer fan') in his World Cup diary, *The Secret World of the Irish Male* (1994).

'We really put on the charm. It became more than football. We became conscious that we were seducing the nations of the world.'

Nell McCafferty.

'The Irish fans start humming the theme tune of the Laurel and Hardy films. This, I am told is because Steve Staunton looks like Stan Laurel, which I really don't think he does.'

Joseph O'Connor, in his World Cup diary, *The Secret World of the Irish Male* (1994).

'So much tension in football, even for these people who don't have to play.'

Jimmy Magee.

'The English were getting harassed all over the place. God love them, with their Union Jacks. They were hounded, frightened and ashamed. We'd ostentatiously give them our Tricolours so that they could put them over their shoulders and get away from the hassle.'

Nell McCafferty.

'They sang it in my ears. Each song in turn to teach me to help me a part of them.'

Marie Jones, *Night in November* (1994).

'I wanted to gee up the players so I went to the touchline and shouted, "Come on" with arms upraised. The noise started with a rumble and built up to a roar and you could feel it building up to a roar.'

Charlie Hurley, on how he inspired one of the most famous renditions of the Dalymount Road may have been invented, Ireland 1 Scotland 0 (9 June 1961).

'FAI now stands for Fans Aren't Important.'

Letter to *The Irish Times*, after the Sky television deal.

'I remember a famous occasion when some of my friends became almost suicidal. In their innocence they flew northwards on a Monday morning in the autumn of 1983, not knowing that Iceland had no pubs. I can still see them wandering around like otters in a land where all the rivers are underground.'

Con Houlihan, *Evening Press* (1989).

'Excuse me, but do Irish people not have televisions in their homes.'

Apocryphal story of an American tourist in a packed hotel during Italia '90. Quoted in John Scally, *Sporting Foot and Mouth* (2002).

'These were the Ireland fans, the loudest and best humoured in the world. Many of these people had followed Ireland all

over the place; they'd seen them being beaten by Trinidad and Tobago and they'd watched example after example of the poxy refereeing that had made playing anywhere more than 10 miles away from Dublin an inevitable misery.'
Roddy Doyle, *The Observer* (1993).

'One per cent of the Irish population was at the game in Stade de France!'
Le Monde, after Ireland v. France at the Stade de France (2004).

1984 (Bohemians)

Blue Till I Die (Waterford)

Down to the River (Finn Harps)

EMFA – Every Man A Football Artist (Kilkenny)

Forza Drogs (Drogheda)

FourFiveOne (Cork United)

Glenmalure Gazette (Shamrock Rovers)

One F In Longford (Longford)

Osam Is Doubtful (St Patrick's Athletic)

Out on a Lim (Limerick)

Red Inc (Shelbourne) still going

STIG (UCD) had its 50th issue recently and is still going

The Tribal Bible (Galway)

Titles of Eircom League fanzines.

'If the fans saw someone who was going close to the edge they'd take him home or sit on him and handle him. Circle him. Circle the wagons. Give wee lectures on how it looks bad for the country. They minded each other a great deal, people who were broke or just too drunk.'

Nell McCafferty.

'When we got to the stadium I looked back down the main avenue and it was packed with orange. But there, right in the middle of it all, was a German policeman on a horse, and on the back of the horse was one Irish supporter, proudly waving the Tricolour. It was a wonderful moment, the Irish were coming.'

Mick McCarthy, on the match against The Netherlands in Gelsenkirchen (1988).

Fields of Dreams

A hundred years ago, soccer playing in Ireland was growing in popularity and proud of its fields, its pavilions, its stands and its infrastructure. Somewhere along the way, they forgot about the spectators and substandard facilities became acceptable. And then somebody sold Glenmalure Park when we weren't looking.

'Dalymount Park is now recognised as one of the finest grounds in these countries. It has a present capacity of 45,000 and will ultimately hold 75,000.'

Programme note (1936).

'Dalymount is plain hell and the Irish the most fanatical crowd of supporters ever known. The crowd are right in on the touchlines, and the police have to marshal them to allow corner kicks to be taken.'

French manager (1953).

'It was just a reminder of how badly we need better accommodation for our soccer followers.'

W. P. Murphy, on Ireland v. France, *Irish Independent* (1953).

'Gates were broken down. Many got in for nothing, the pitch was inundated any time of note occurred or when there was a stoppage in play giving the youth of Dublin a chance to show how undisciplined they are.'

W. P. Murphy, on Ireland v. Austria, *Irish Independent* (1963).

'One friendly stands out. 1985. Dalymount Park, a dank, generally empty Stalinist concrete stadium. Irish soccer is at such a low ebb that when Italy visit as World Champions nobody bothers issuing tickets to the game.'

Dermot Bolger.

'A potato patch.'

Italian newspaper, describing scenes at Dalymount after a friendly match between Ireland and Italy (1985).

'Their removal from the Woodbrook Ground to the Carlisle Grounds has result in greater support and with a change of jerseys this year are hoping to bring with it a change of luck.'

Bray Unknowns, programme note (1936).

'A smelly ditch along the Swan River.'

Deirdre Kelly, describing the original Lansdowne Road, *Four Roads to Dublin* (1996).

'What is the difference between a state-of-the-art sports stadium in Japan and a state-of-the-art sports stadium in Ireland? The Japanese get a retractable pitch; the Irish get a retractable stadium.'

Letter to *The Irish Times*, during 2002 World Cup finals.

'South Korea 10 Ireland 0.'

Irish Independent, pondering the matter of building football stadiums.

'For the more sophisticated European teams it wasn't just our primitive style that bemused or terrified them. Lansdowne Road was a rugby pitch and played like one, particularly when the wear and tear of a rugby season left the pitch bare and rutted. This made the fluent pass-and-move football game favoured by the better sides difficult, if not impossible, to play.'

Roy Keane, *The Autobiography* (2002).

'They are rapidly developing their grounds Glenmalure Park, Miltown, which is one of the best in the city and has now a splendid clubhouse installed.'

Programme note (1936).

'The Tramway End is a dangerous place for a young boy alone, especially when Ireland score and bodies cascade down the steps in celebration. Fortunately for my health, Ireland rarely score and we've nothing to celebrate. At least I learn the truth early on. Following Ireland is an obsession with nothing to do with enjoyment.'

Dermot Bolger.

'Smaller stadia in Oslo were upgraded at a time when the owners of Shamrock Rovers were selling Milltown to property developers. As a result, the Norwegian league has a top side in Rosenborg. The clear message for domestic brands is that they can thrive in the face of huge competition, but they have to be managed carefully and marketed assiduously.'

David McWilliams, economist.

'Ireland's home games were played at Lansdowne Road, a rugby pitch, a bumpy disgrace, or at Dalymount, where they had to cut the grass on the roof of the stand at the start of every season.'

Roddy Doyle.

'I'm not saying the game lacked atmosphere, but you could hear the corpses in Glasnevin cemetery during the second half.'

Damien Richardson, writing after a match in Whitehall.

'If the man with the hose was good enough for Athlone, he was good enough for AC Milan.'

Declan Lynch, on the day AC Milan came to St Mel's Park to play in the UEFA Cup (1975). The Italians were appalled to find there were no working showers at the grounds.

Find an Irishman:
The FAI's Cunning Plan

Confined to minority status and a clearly defined urban area, Irish soccer discovered a way out of the constraints of its geography in the 1960s. FIFA parentage rules gave it access to the million or so members of the Irish community living in England, who grew up in a soccer culture and who had learned to play the game at a high level. It was instantly successful in boosting the game in Ireland, and set a precedent which basketball has since followed with American-born players. Ireland is not alone in recruiting this way; it was the fact that the foreign-born soon overwhelmed the home-growns that provided endless fascination for English commentators. It is good fun trying to figure out which was the most tenuously connected Irishman – a lead candidate would by Tommy Coyne, who qualified through his great-grandmother. Under FIFA rules, if they had existed at the time, James Connolly and Eamon de Valera would have been eligible to play for Ireland – as would Alfredo de Stefano.

'Qualification shall be by birth within the area of the national association. In the case of subjects from abroad, their nationality shall be decided by the nationality of their fathers.'

England's proposed rule change given at the 1962 FIFA Congress.

'All players have to be citizens of the country for which they have declared.'

FIFA rules (1995).

'Biggest ambition: To play for England.'

Michael Robinson, in a questionnaire for *Shoot* magazine. Between the time the magazine went to press and went on sale, he had been called up for Ireland.

'All I have to do now is get the accent right.'

Clinton Morrison (2001).

'My grandmother's name is Joyce, but I don't know her surname and I don't know where she is from in Ireland. I met her once but I don't know if she is alive.'

Marlon King, making his case for the Irish team (2001).

'Six of the team wearing green that night were born in England. A seventh, Ray Houghton, was born in Scotland. Our manager Jack Charlton was one of the most famous English footballers of all time.'

Tony Cascarino, talking about Ireland v. Italy in the 1990 World Cup finals, *Full Time: The Secret Life of Tony Cascarino* (2000).

'I thought of my uncles and my aunts scattered through England and the United States, of every generation culled and shipped off by beef by the hoof. And suddenly it seemed they had found a voice at last, that the Houghtons and McCarthys were playing for all those generations written out of history. And I knew they were playing for my children to come too, for Shane's and Mick's, who would grow up with foreign accents and Irish faces, bewildered by their fathers' lives.'

Dermot Bolger, *In High Germany*, a play set during the 1988 European Championship finals (1990).

'For those countries with diasporas like Scotland and Ireland, it adds a sense of history and romance to the cynical pot of modern sport. They are coming home.'

Nicky Campbell (October 2005).

'My mum wasn't an O'Malley as I'd always believed. I didn't qualify for Ireland. I was a fraud. A fake Irishman. Writing this book has been a very difficult experience. But it was also good therapy for me. I don't know how people are going to take it or what's going to happen now. But I'd want people to know that I'm very proud to consider myself Irish.'

Tony Cascarino, *Full Time: The Secret Life of Tony Cascarino* (2000).

'Tony has created a bit of a mess for himself, it will cloud people's memories. There was no reason to say it. There was no reason to admit it. Why did he have to mention it in the first place? When Tony found out four years ago that he wasn't qualified to play for Ireland, he should have told the FAI. It was a troublesome situation and he should have sat down with them and discussed it. It would have been difficult, but it would have been the right thing to do.'

Jack Charlton.

'I don't know what he could have done in 1996 when he found out that there might be a problem. He had already got 60-oddcaps at that stage and he was given an Irish passport so that indicated he did qualify.'

Mick McCarthy.

'However irritating and irrelevant at one level, the Cascarino story is a useful reminder of something important. The tale of Tony's roots imparts a useful moral. Irishness is not a simple concept.'

Fintan O'Toole, journalist, *The Irish Times*.

'Most of us suspect the [Cascarino] controversy was orchestrated to promote his book. Good on ya, Cas. Now that's really Irish.'

Paddy Clancy, *The Sun* (Irish edition).

'When Bernard O'Byrne became FAI Chief Executive on October 1, 1996, neither Tony Cascarino, John Aldridge nor Jason McAteer had an Irish passport. All three travelled on British passports, although Aldridge was adamant last night that he was issued with an Irish one before he made his international debut in 1986.'

Philip Quinn, sportswriter.

'What can they have been thinking of with the decision to play a World Cup game in Belfast? For a start the connections between the team calling itself 'Ireland' and this country are fairly nebulous. With only one bona fide Irish-born player on the team the only real surprise is that nobody asked Tony Cascarino to come out of international retirement and play at full-back.'

Des Fahy, writing on the decision to stage the rugby league World Cup fixtures in Belfast, *The Irish Times* (2001).

'John Aldridge or Tony Cascarino were as Irish as the Tower of London, but it was possible for our imaginations to accept them as Irishmen-of-convenience, in a way which wouldn't really be possible with a Russian or a German.'

Kevin Myers, columnist, *The Irish Times*.

'If you have a fortnight's holiday in Dublin you qualify for an Irish cap.'

Mike England, Wales manager and Jack Charlton's first opponent as Ireland manager, talking before the sides met (1986).

'I want to play for Ireland. I qualify because I flew on Aer Lingus once.'

Jimmy Greaves.

'Greg Rusedski? Who's he? If you are going to find a Brit you might as well go for the best. Jack Charlton would have got us Pete Sampras.'

Des Lynam, Clare-born TV presenter.

'Because you have made a different life for yourself in another country, that doesn't make you any less Irish.'
Steve Staunton (2001).

'I would be faced with the choice of playing for Russia, the Ukraine or Lithuania, all of which I am eligible for. It was also possible that I was eligible for France. Someone even told me that Jack Charlton had made enquiries to see if I had great-grandparents with Irish blood.'
Andrei Kanchelskis, on the break-up of the old Soviet Union.

'They may not all have been born in Ireland, but they had their roots in the country, had economic circumstances not forced their ancestors to emigrate, they would have grown up and worked in Ireland. The fact that it didn't work out like that made them no less Irish.'
Jack Charlton (1994).

'The English-born players didn't need to sing The Furey Brothers for us to appreciate them.'
Niall Quinn (2001).

'I'd be delighted if Stan Collymore is eligible for Ireland because our agreement with Southend is that we pay them more if he plays for England.'
Frank Clark (1994).

'It's easy enough to get to Ireland. It's just a straight walk across the Irish Sea as far as I am concerned.'
Brian Clough, announcing his interest in the Irish job (1995).

'Liam George would have been captain under Jack Charlton, he has an English accent, he has dreadlocks and his face is black.'

Brian Kerr.

'Bobby Robson's would-be champions of Europe were scuttled by a bunch of international mercenaries recruited from their own First Division. Goalscorer Ray Houghton, a Glaswegian, and Jack Charlton, an Englishman.'

Daily Mail, reporting on Ireland v. England in the Euro '88 Championship.

'A lot of Jack's players are happy to be picked up for the Republic because they couldn't find a way of making it with England or Scotland.'

Billy Bingham, Northern Ireland manager.

'What Billy said is a scandal. When I was first picked for Ireland it was not just the pounds sign which flashed before my eyes, but the shamrock.'

John Aldridge.

'Nanna from heaven for Jack Charlton.'

Nicky Campbell, *The Guardian* (6 October 2005).

'With McBride and Donovan and O'Brien we should be supporting them.'

Liam Brady, on the USA team that reached the 2002 World Cup quarter-final.

'I had two passports, one for football and the real one.'

Sean Fallon, explaining how he took four years off his age in the hope of getting a deal with Glasgow Celtic.

'The mongrel nature of the team from Glasgow, London and Manchester, as well as from Irish towns and cities is the best representation of what it means to be Irish now. And for a substantial part of the team's following which is made up of emigrants, major championships offer the possibility of belonging for a few weeks to an Ireland conjured up on foreign soil.'

Fintan O'Toole (1993).

'Half of them's English that weren't good enough to play for England and then they discover some oul Irish bog woman that was meant too be their granny, They never set foot in Ireland before, wouldn't have known a shillelagh from a hole in the wall and now, be Jesus, you'd think they were after starting the 1916 Rising.'

Lead character in *Night in November* by Marie Jones, a play about a Belfast Loyalist who ends up supporting the Irish football team (1994).

'The English league is becoming a training ground for other teams' World Cup squads.'

Jimmy Armfield, former England international.

'A true football fan is one who knows the nationality of every Republic of Ireland player.'

Ken Bolam, English musician (1996).

George Best

Within days of George Best's death, there was talk of monuments being erected and airports being named in his honour. Disarmingly shy before he became the greatest sporting celebrity this country has produced, it seemed that his talent, his skill and his life passed him, leaving us all to mourn for lost talent, lost youth, lost innocence, and the capacity to live life to the full and perhaps beyond. 'Where did it all go wrong?' indeed.

'They'll forget all the rubbish when I've gone and they'll remember the football. If only one person thinks I'm the best player in the world, that's good enough for me.'
George Best, *Blessed: The Autobiography* (2002).

'The good, the bad and the bubbly.'
Title of George Best autobiography (1991).

'I spent a lot of my money on booze, birds and fast cars. The rest I just squandered.'

George Best.

'George, where did it all go wrong?'

Apocryphal story of what a waiter said to George Best when he was delivering room service. Over twenty versions of the story have been tracked by a Manchester museum. The best-known has George in a hotel bedroom with Miss World, champagne and a night's casino winnings spread across the bed when the question was asked.

'When I was a kid the only thing I shared my bed with was a football. I used to take the ball to bed with me. I know it sounds daft but I used to love the feel of it. I used to hold it, look at it and think: One day you'll do everything I tell you.'

George Best.

'If you want the secret of my success with women, then don't smoke, don't take drugs and don't be too particular.'

George Best.

'I'd have to be a superman to do all the things I am supposed to have done. I've been in six different places at six different times.'

George Best.

'I always had a reputation for going missing, Miss England, Miss United Kingdom, Miss World.'

George Best (1992).

'They say I've slept with seven Miss Worlds. I didn't. It was only four. I didn't turn up for the other three.'
George Best.

Interviewer: 'What would you do if you weren't a footballer?'
George Best: 'Manage the Miss World contest. I might get the four birds I missed.'

'If you'd given me a choice of beating four men and smashing in a goal from 30 yards against Liverpool or going to bed with Miss World, it would have been a difficult choice. Luckily I had both. It's just that you do one of those things in front of 50,000 people.'
George Best (1991).

'Once I started playing football I realised I was in the perfect position for pulling birds. I had the limelight, the publicity, the money. Where could I go wrong?'
George Best.

'Mary Stavin is the only woman to whom I was almost always faithful.'
George Best.

'Having a baby is a big thing. We would like three, one of each.'
George Best, speaking when he was married to Alex.

'I've stopped drinking, but only while I'm asleep.'
George Best.

'Once you get a taste of George Best, you never want to taste another thing.'

Alex Best (1979).

'He's one of the most intelligent considerate and generous of men. I still love him, but there are problems better solved on his own.'

Mary Stavin, speaking as she left Best.

'Just as I wanted to outdo everyone when I played, I had to outdo everyone when we were on the town always the last to go home.'

George Best.

In 1969 I gave up women and alcohol – it was the worst 20 minutes of my life.'

George Best.

'I don't drink every day, but when I do it's usually for four or five days on the trot.'

George Best.

'Just my luck, they gave me George Best's liver.'

Jim Baxter, former Rangers player, after a liver transplant failed.

'When he is boozing he is the most deplorable, obnoxious, sarcastic, ignorant, horrible piece of rubbish.'

Alex Best.

'It took a lot of bottle for George to own up.'
Ian Wright, on Best's confession to alcoholism.

Michael Parkinson: 'What was the nearest to kick-off that you made love to a woman?'
George Best: 'Er – I think it was half-time actually.'

'I might go to Alcoholics Anonymous, but I think it'd be difficult for me to be anonymous.'
George Best (1980).

'I saw a sign saying: "Drink Canada Dry."'
George Best, explaining why he went to America.

'Alcohol controls me. It's a disease and has nothing to do with me personally. I never go a day without thinking about drinking.'
George Best (1990).

'Sometimes I feel like a one man zoo.'
George Best.

'Most of the things I have done have been my own fault so I can't feel guilty about them.'
George Best.

'I was in for 10 hours and had 40 pints – beating my previous record by 20 minutes.
George Best, talking about a blood transfusion for his liver transplant, not on his drinking.

'People always say I should not be burning the candle at both ends. Maybe because they don't have a big enough candle.'
George Best.

'If George had been born ugly, he probably would have played till he was 40... just look at Peter Beardsley.'
Paddy Crerand, paying tribute to George Best (January 2000).

'George is in good spirits.'
Philip Hughes, George Best's spokesman, giving an unfortunately worded progress report on Best's recovery from liver problems (April 2000).

'You can't get any lower than that, unless you're dead. I went there and had a good look at myself. I thought: "What the hell are you doing to yourself, what's happening?" I decided from then on, that I was going to work hard and get myself sorted out.'
George Best, on landing in prison (December 1984).

'El Beatle.'
Portuguese headline after Manchester United's 5-1 win over Benfica gave birth to the Best legend (1966).

'The game in Portugal for me was something of a starting point. That was probably the occasion when I decided it was only going to get better. From that match on I actually believed there was nobody better than me. It is amazing what one performance can do.'
George Best, on the 5-1 defeat of Benfica.

'Perhaps it is simply because I have got older, but the soccer scene today doesn't excite me as much as when I made my debut eight years ago. Everything was new and exciting. I believe that my job is to entertain the people who paid money to see me play. One of the big problems with modern-day soccer is that it has become too stereotyped with everyone preoccupied by defence.'
George Best (1972).

'I was right footed to start with but I worked harder on my left and it became better than my right. It annoys me today when I see players who can't kick with both feet.'
George Best, on his fiftieth birthday (1996).

'A lot of rubbish is talked about destroyers and tough defenders. I call them dirty b–ds.'
George Best.

'If a fellow has to kick me, it means he is not as good as I am.'
George Best.

'Every team had a hard man. We had Nobby Stiles. Chelsea had Chopper. Arsenal had Peter Storey. Liverpool had Tommy Smith. Leeds had eleven of them.'
George Best.

'Do they seriously think I don't want to change. Of course I do. But I can't change. I know myself well enough to realise I can't promise the change. I can only try and go on trying. I can get whacked from the back or hit when the ball has gone 28 times in a row and do nothing or say nothing. I don't know why it should boil the 29th time, which has been no different. It just happens.'

George Best.

'I don't really class myself as a footballer. I call myself an entertainer.'

George Best.

'When I'm on the field nothing gives me more pleasure than making a fool of somebody.'

George Best.

'Football cut George Best off at adolescence.'

Malcolm Allison.

'I never subscribed to Alf Ramsey's doctrine of hard running off the ball. I am a footballer and that means having a football at my feet.'

George Best.

'To call Keegan a superstar is stretching a point. Kevin Keegan is not fit to lace my boots.'

George Best

'Keegan is not fit to lace George Best's drinks.'

John Roberts, journalist.

'He's not George Best, but then, no one is.'

Clive Tyldesley.

'There's no way Ryan Giggs is another George Best. He's another Ryan Giggs.'

Denis Law.

'When Geoff Thomas traps the ball it goes as far as I used to be able to kick it.'

George Best.

'Paul Gascoigne is being accused of being arrogant, unable to cope with the press, and a boozer. Sounds like he's got a chance to me.'

George Best.

'He wears No 10. I thought it was his position, but it turns out it is his IQ.'

George Best, on Paul Gascoigne.

'I'd be surprised if all 22 players are on the field at the end of the game – one's already been sent off.'

George Best.

'I don't think he's a great player. He can't kick with his left foot, he doesn't score many goals, he can't head a ball and he can't tackle. Apart from that he's all right.'

George Best, on David Beckham (January 2000).

'When George came to Manchester United he couldn't pull a bird. We used to give him our cast-offs. He never returned the compliment.'

Eamon Dunphy, on George Best.

'There's a lot of advice for people. If they had told me how to behave I would probably have done the opposite.'
George Best.

'He has three problems, he is famous, he is rich and he is Irish. Not a good combination.'
Peter Stringfellow.

'He was Roy of the Rovers on the field but Roy of the Ravers off it.'
International Hall of Fame website, describing George Best (2000).

'It was typical of me to be finishing drinking just as the English government is thinking of opening pubs 24 hours a day.'
George Best (2001).

'It's a pleasure for me to be standing up here. It's a pleasure for me to be standing up.'
George Best accepting the Footballer of the Century Award (1999).

'They tell me to do so many things. So many bloody things. Shave my beard, cut my hair, as if that would make me into what they want me to be. Jesus Christ had a beard and long hair they didn't want to change him.'
George Best.

'Everybody makes mistakes. Mine just seem to get more publicity than everyone else's.'

George Best.

'I don't have many regrets. If there is one big one, it is leaving United as early as I did because I could have become a multi-millionaire. Too bad, but at the time I just couldn't handle it. The pressure was just too much for me.'

George Best.

Gilesie:

The Founding Father

There was soccer in Ireland before John Giles. It was a simpler game, they were simpler times, and the rejection and reawakening he underwent after being dropped in 1969 caused less national trauma than that of Roy Keane a few decades later. When he became player-manager of the Irish team in circumstances and at an age that will never be repeated, he reinvented the way we looked at the world and made success possible.

'The only reason I took the job was that if I did not do it, it might go to someone I did not rate that much.'

John Giles, on become Irish team manager at the age of 32 (1973).

'I thought it was about time something was done about the situation. We couldn't keep going the way we were. We drafted a statement and went to the FAI. It was the start of the breakdown of the selection committee.'

John Giles, on the quiet revolution in Irish soccer that occurred in 1969.

'John told us we could become a world force. When he left we knew we could be.'

Eamon Dunphy.

'Giles was the man everybody wanted to sort out. He was extremely adept at escaping bookings. He would be furthest away when anything went off. And he was nearly always the instigator.'

Terry Conroy of Stoke City, capped 26 times for Ireland.

'I told Don Revie I was dropped and he said, "They must have some selection of players."'

John Giles on how he was dropped by Ireland for one of the qualifiers for the 1970 World Cup finals – in favour of Eamon Dunphy.

'1973. We win a match, against Germany's youths or the mothers of German players – I can't remember, just that it's a rare victory. John Giles takes over.'

Dermot Bolger.

'That would be hard from the substitutes' bench.'

John Giles answers Eoin Hand's question of whether he was needed to go forward for corner kicks against USSR (1974).

It was the first Hand knew that he was being dropped to make way for Liam Brady.

'At least we were disappointed.'

John Giles, talking after defeat in Berne ended Ireland's European Championship dreams, the first time in eleven years Ireland had seriously contended for a place in the finals (1975).

'There are two fallacies about his style of play. Number one is that everyone had to give the ball to Giles. That was nonsense. More often than not he was the first available player which is why he got it. Fallacy number two concerned passing the ball backwards. I worked longer with John Giles than anyone and he never said pass the ball backwards.'

Ray Treacy, quoted in Sean Ryan, *The Boys in Green* (1997).

'John Giles has become manager now, and has recalled me to the squad after a two-year absence. Which is great. But when I went to see Benny today for permission to go, he really hummed and hawed. He kept raising objections because we have the League Cup replay against Forest next Wednesday.'

Eamon Dunphy, *Only a Game* (1976).

'A young man of real ability would have top think twice about a career in English soccer management. Who would be judging his work? Amateurs mostly.'

Johnny Giles (1981).

'In the last 10 months, 33 League clubs have changed managers. The directors have power without responsibility.

The government should issue a health warning to managers: The only certain thing is the sack.'
Johnny Giles (1977).

'The Catholic Church abolished limbo, but they never told John Giles and his former Leeds manager who staged the worst testimonial game ever in Lansdowne Road.'
Dermot Bolger.

'Johnny Giles was the kindest man to a friend. But Johnny didn't have many friends.'
Ray Treacy, quoted in Paul Rowan, *The Team That Jack Built* (1994).

'Giles like St Patrick when he was in Gaul, had heard voices and was coming over to convert the Irish.'
Con Houlihan, *Evening Press*.

'He's gone to count the money.'
Overheard at Giles' testimonial match in Lansdowne Road, an abysmal 0-0 draw.

'I always had confidence in my football but I wasn't much confident in anything else. I was very shy and a very self-conscious type of young fellow.'
John Giles, quoted in Colm Keane, *Ireland's Soccer Top Twenty* (2004).

'What did me a lot of harm is that I came back to Shamrock Rovers and familiarity breeds contempt.'
John Giles.

'Nobody ever expected us to qualify for European Championships or World Cups. What I did was to raise the expectancy. It was my own downfall in long run because after three or four championships they said, "Ah Giles is no good."'

John Giles, quoted in Colm Keane, *Ireland's Soccer Top Twenty* (2004).

'Unfortunately for us the way things were going, it was the worst thing that could happen. It only encouraged the FAI to go on the way they were going.'

John Giles, after Ireland qualified for the quarter-finals of the 1964 European Championship.

'The main thing when I took over the Irish team was to get over the inferiority complex of those days. I always got the feeling it was okay for everyone else to do it but not okay for us to do it.'

John Giles, quoted in Colm Keane, *Ireland's Soccer Top Twenty* (2004).

'I thought I might as well do it myself rather than somebody else do it and do it who's not going to do it in the way I think it should be done.'

John Giles, on being asked to manage the Irish team at the age of 32, quoted in Paul Rowan, *The Team That Jack Built* (1994).

'People thought I was a highly paid guy who enjoyed the publicity surrounding it. I never did. When you become national team manager you become public property. Once the people around me became affected by it, I said I would stop doing it. And I never missed it.'

John Giles.

'Over the years we had loads of moral victories because people expected that. We went away and we were beaten 2–0 and it was a good performance, a moral victory.'

John Giles, quoted in Colm Keane, *Ireland's Soccer Top Twenty* (2004).

Journalist: 'We're not winning the vital matches.'

Eamon Dunphy: 'We've not been playing the vital matches before.'

Exchange at Ireland training session before match against Denmark in 1979 recorded by Peter Ball, *Magill*. [Dunphy?]

'I wasn't playing badly. It was just an image thing. I didn't handle things well. I was a bit of a smart arse.'

John Giles, quoted in Paul Rowan, *The Team That Jack Built* (1994).

'Usually it takes a bottle of Bacardi and a gallon of coke to get John out of his seat.'

Eamon Dunphy.

Gloom and Doom

For Irish soccer followers of a certain age, there have been more defeats than victories. As fans of the bad football pun love to remind us – life is a pitch.

'Yesterday the unthinkable happened. Ireland drew with a mountain top.'
Peter Ball, reporting on Ireland's 0–0 draw with Liechtenstein, *Sunday Tribune* (1995).

'There's nothing I can do for you. You will have to work this one out for yourselves.'
Jack Charlton, during his half-time team talk in the match against Liechtenstein (1995).

'When the golden goal went in, it was like doing 10 years in prison and then walking out and getting a smack of a bus.'
Gerry Smith, Ireland manager, after Ireland fought back from

2–0 down to Colombia, only to lose to a golden goal at the
World Youth Cup (2003)

'There are good things coming for this club.'

David Crawley, Dundalk's captain, after winning the FAI
Cup final and being relegated from the Premier Division of
the National League the previous week.

'It was so frustrating and when Frei came over giving it large
in front of our bench I thought: "I'm not having that." That's
when I threw the bottle on the pitch. Everything about their
celebration seemed to be about winding us up.'

Mark Kinsella, former Republic of Ireland international, on
the crucial defeat in the Euro 2004 campaign in Basle.

'I'm not going on in that rain.'

Andy McEvoy of Limerick, responding to a request to go on
the field during a World Cup qualifier in Prague (1969).
Ireland lost 3–0.

'I almost walked away. I thought to myself: "You've bought a
club in the back of beyond, with Nanouk the Eskimo as your
nearest neighbour, and it's a shambles – do you really need
this?"'

John Courtenay, on becoming chairman at Carlisle United.

'Like in all cycles, it's reality come back to haunt us. My
footballing memory of 1997 wasn't something that happened
on the pitch, it was trying to console my eight year old who
took to the bed after Ireland were knocked out by Belgium.
I looked at his bowed head. I didn't just want to console him,

I wanted to shield him from the terrible truth that fathers in small nations must tell their children. "If God spares you, you'll have another eighty or ninety years of matches like this to endure."'

Dermot Bolger.

'Frank Stapleton smiles in the mirror first thing every morning, just to get it over with.'

Ron Atkinson.

'We were very close. We had a couple of dreadful refereeing decisions in Bulgaria and France. But people didn't want to know about that.'

John Giles, quoted in Colm Keane, *Ireland's Soccer Top Twenty* (2004).

'We don't care anymore. We don't care what happens. The FAI have their investigating to do and doubtless it will be unseemly. There are a few shouting matches left to be had. They'll be ugly too. But Niigata, Ibaraki, Yokohama and Suwon. They are the memories to insulate us. The World Cup is just a TV show now and the bunting is beginning to fade in the wind, but we can wonder if it's worth packing it away again; the good times will be back, and soon.'

Tom Humphries, on Ireland's exit from the World Cup finals, *The Irish Times* (2002).

'What I tried to instil into the players more than anything else was an expectancy to win. We're not going to win every match but if you deserve to win it, you win it. I'd played in the Irish team over the years where you would go in afterwards and you'd say, "They weren't so good after all. We could have done them."'

John Giles, quoted in Paul Rowan, *The Team That Jack Built* (1994).

'There was a lot of criticism, a lot of hostility, and my attitude was: I don't need this. I was doing my best for the Irish team and I am not getting the reaction. The team wasn't losing.'

John Giles, quoted in Paul Rowan, *The Team That Jack Built* (1994).

'I thought the second match, the one we won, was the one against Trinidad and Tobago.'

Eamonn Deacy, interviewed a decade after the farcical tour of South America in 1982. Ireland lost 1-0 to Chile, 7-0 to Brazil and 2-1 to Trinidad and Tobago. They then beat a Trinidadian club side 2-1.

'No wonder we lost. We had to play both Trinidad and Tobago.'

Irish fan.

Green:

All Forty Shades of It

International soccer is one of the few forums where flags, anthems and nationalities still matter. The evolution of Ireland since the 1870s has been dramatic, complex and often unexpected, as can be told by the reactions of those who have worn the green, white, blue and even orange jersey on behalf of Ireland on soccer fields in five continents. And also from their fans, camp-followers and those who have watched the process.

'I hope our one is not as long.'
Terry Mancini, after the Irish national anthem was played on his debut against Poland – he hadn't recognised it (1973).

'The FAI has lodged an official complaint with FIFA about the official Irish flag that has been used at the games. It's the wrong colour. And so, it's the wrong flag. FIFA has supplied one which is green, white and a particularly insipid yellow. Yellow is not orange. The FAI has been fielding complaints in Dublin from viewers, at home and overseas, about this.'

Miriam Lord, journalist, describing a diplomatic incident during the 2002 World Cup finals.

'We are a decade or so into the country's Celtic Tiger phenomenon and maybe that has made us a more demanding nation.'

Niall Quinn, *The Guardian* (7 October 2005).

'What you have to understand about we Irishmen is that we are naturally very loyal people.'

Charlie Hurley.

'When I started out playing for Ireland the manager was Jack Charlton and the criticism was that we played caveman football. There was an element of truth to that and I would not apologise for it because I always felt that the sheer urgency of our play somehow contained a degree of our Irishness. We are the country of Gaelic football, of hurling; we are not Holland.'

Niall Quinn, *The Guardian* (7 October 2005).

'Little Ireland now stand on the threshold of becoming one of the elite of European soccer. But jeering is hardly the way to encourage them to success. Have the soccer-going public here been so well off that they can afford to cock a snoot at success?

Mel Moffatt, *Irish Press* (12 May 1975).

'Why does the Irish national anthem ended with the line: "Shoving Connie around the field."'
American fan at the World Cup finals in America (1994).

'It was funny that one of Ireland's greatest football achievements actually lacked drama. Who would have foreseen the day when Ireland would stroll into the last sixteen of the World Cup?'
Mark Lawrenson, speaking about the 2002 World Cup finals.

'It's better being the underdog, don't you think? Nobody's being a killjoy, but favouritism doesn't rest easily on our shoulders. It never has (ref: Egypt, Liechtenstein, Andorra etc).'
Andy Townsend.

'Is this a football match or a crowd of lions waiting for the Christians.'
Marie Jones, *Night in November* (1994).

'It was a victory over selfishness, ego and begrudgery. It was a victory not just for a team but a nation. And it was as Irish as the earlier defeat of France by Denmark had been utterly French.'
Editorial in the *Irish Independent,* on Ireland's qualification for the last sixteen of the World Cup finals (2002).

'They arrived at the tournament a seemingly nondescript bunch and left it a serious international team. Just doomed in the end by penalties.'
Vincent Hogan, *Irish Independent.*

'The country also needs to be able also to express its collective gratitude to the team, not just for the performance on the soccer pitch but what they have achieved for the national psyche – for enhancing our camaraderie, for renewing our national pride but above all for bringing happiness.'

Patricia Casey, psychologist.

'In the previous two World Cups, we were grateful to the team for what they didn't do: screw up and make a show of us. This time, we can show our gratitude for what they actually did. They reminded us that the values of an older society don't have to be ditched for the energies of a new one. It is perhaps appropriate that a frightened officialdom should treat them like toxic waste, corralling their homecoming into a safe space on the edge of the city.'

Fintan O'Toole, journalist, on Ireland's performance in the 2002 World Cup finals.

'Now we can play world-class football, surely we no longer need to celebrate when we lose.'

Róisín Ingle, journalist, on Ireland's performance in the 2002 World Cup finals.

'Throughout my career I have been called a rebel, a show-off, a belligerent non-conformist, a trouble-maker and a few unrepeatable names usually prefaced with the tag Irish which is supposed to explain, if not absolve, everything.'

Derek Dougan, in his autobiography *Attack* (1969).

'When our teams go away for international games, when they go to France, Belgium, England or Scotland, they perform a useful function to this State. Are they not an international advertisement for this State?'

J. J. Byrne, debate in Dáil Éireann (July 1931).

'The encouragement of association football is in the interests of the country. It is not alone in the interests of those who play association football, but it is in the national interests. Anybody who takes the view that Gaelic football is more a national game than association football is taking an extremely narrow view.'

J. J. Byrne, debate in Dáil Éireann (July 1931).

'The proliferation of soccer on this island is the best thing that has happened since the arrival of the potato.'

Con Houlihan, *Evening Press* (May 1989).

'Look at the Irish. They sing their national anthem and none of them know the words. Jack Charlton sings, and all he knows is Cushy Butterfield and Blaydon Races. But look at the pride they have in those green shirts.'

Lawrie McMenemy.

'Jud-as, Jud-as.'

English fans' chant directed at Jack Charlton.

'The country had been ravaged by the most contagious fever since the foundation of the state. Football fever. Blotched in green white and orange, we could not have been greeted more fervently if we'd won.'

Tony Cascarino, *Full Time: The Secret Life of Tony Cascarino* (2000).

'The first bars ring out. I notice the TV camera start to zoom in. Should I move my lips and sing the two or three lines that I know?'

Andy Townsend, *Andy's Game* (1994).

'The more time I spend with him, the more Irish I feel.'

Bobby Robson, on his ITV co-pundit Andy Townsend.

'We have never had it easy, you know. Windsor Park, Poland, Anfield, they were all cup finals.'

Mick Byrne, Irish team physio.

'We Irish have found it hard to let go of our anti-English prejudices. Especially as they have given us such perverse pleasure over the years, when we had nothing else.'

Declan Lynch (2004).

'Come on Norn Iron. Come on.'

Northern Ireland Development Board ad screened at time of 1982 World Cup finals.

'And when they were gone, we turned, solid to a man and a woman, thirteen thousand of us, cheering, applauding, chanting out the players' names, letting them know how proud we felt. I thought of my father's battered travel-light bag, of Molloy drilling us behind that 1798 pike, the wasters who came after him hammering Peig into us, the masked men blowing limbs of passers-by off in my name. You know, all my life it seems that somebody somewhere has always been trying to tell me what Ireland I belong to. But I only belonged there. I raised my hands and applauded, having finally, in my last moments with Shane and Mick found the only Ireland whose name I can sing, given to me by eleven men dressed in green. And the only Ireland I can pass on to the son who will carry my name and features in a foreign land.'

Dermot Bolger, *In High Germany*, a play set during the 1988 European Championship finals (1990).

'How could I play against England. I'd supported England as a boy. England was my team. The land of my birth. But that's exactly what transpired.'

Tony Cascarino, *Full Time: The Secret Life of Tony Cascarino* (2000).

'1973: Ireland celebrate the closest thing we have to footballing success – England's failure to reach the World Cup finals. They're knocked out at Wembley by the majestic goalkeeping skills of Poland's Tomaszewski. Next day Tomaszewski and the other Poles arrive in Dublin for a friendly and, to their utter bewilderment, discover they are national heroes. They are serenaded with Polish music on *The Late Late Show*. Nymphs and virgins would be strewn at their feet if nymphs and virgins could have been found in time. Finally, glazed and hung over, they reach Dalymount and we hockey them 1–0. Irish players return to silent dressing rooms in lowly second division clubs and hang up swapped Polish jerseys. It may not have felt as good as Stuttgart but in those days it was as close as we got.'

Dermot Bolger.

'Most international studies of human happiness show that the average Irish person derives 63 per cent of his or her sense of well-being from watching England losing football matches. These figures have remained consistent for centuries until a few weeks ago, when, for some mysterious reason, something changed ... Something has changed for ever in the relationship between Ireland and England. Something that we have cherished is no more. The fact of the matter is, that when England were playing Argentina at this World Cup, I felt different about it. I felt like I wanted England to... how can I put this?... to not lose, and maybe even to... I think the technical term is – to win.'

Declan Lynch (June 2002).

'Rugby and soccer people are sick and tired of having the finger pointed at him as if they were any worse Irishmen for playing these games. When Ireland was asked for sons to call to the colours we were there and were not asked what shape of a ball we used.'

Donough O'Malley, Minister for Education (1968).

'I am a follower of the League of Ireland, a position analogous to being an adherent of a minority religion which, like Bahai, Lutheranism or Seventh Day Adventism, is big enough for survival but far too small to really thrive. Soccer in Ireland is in a pretty unique position. It's hard to think of anywhere else in the world where the mere playing of the game has been decried by others an anti-national act of treachery. The Ban, which was eventually abolished in 1971, forbade members of the Gaelic Athletic Association to play soccer or rugby on pain of expulsion from the association. The GAA's sports of Gaelic football and hurling may have been far more popular than rugby or soccer but, in the spirit of the American blockade of Cuba, they were taking no chances all the same.'

Eamonn Sweeney.

'TNT (Overnight) Irish Cup.'

Sponsored name of Northern Ireland FA Cup at the height of the Troubles.

'Famous Fried Chicken League of Ireland.'

Sponsored name of predecessor of Irish National League in the 1980s.

'When Athlone Town played Finn Harps in the FAI Cup semi-final in Oriel Park, we saw things that day that no one should see. We saw the colourful Athlone goalkeeper Mick O'Brien swinging from the crossbar and breaking it. Twice. And some of us can still hear the public address announcement: "Is there a carpenter in the ground?" RTÉ had some sort of a black-and-white camera at the match, and soon these harrowing images were being screened on English television. They were all laughing at us.'

Declan Lynch.

'The children of the diaspora were included for the first time in a more generous definition of what being Irish means. Young black men could be accepted as part of what we are. An archetypal Englishman, Jack Charlton, became an Irish hero. It is no exaggeration to say that the success of Charlton's teams did more to open up Irish identity than a thousand historical essays or a million political speeches.'

Fintan O'Toole (2001).

'We've got to get from them their biggest ambition, their biggest motivation, they've got to want to play for the green shirt and drop until they're dead.'

Bobby Robson, on becoming consultant to Steve Staunton on the Irish management team (2006).

'I do like playing for Éire, but I need the rest.'

Steve Heighway, when approached to take part in a 1972 tour to Brazil.

'The media of every nation on earth is unacceptably, disgracefully, triumphalist about the success of their national team. To single out the English is completely silly. Even if the English media has been unacceptably, disgracefully triumphalist about the Irish team.'

Declan Lynch (June 2002).

'Eoin Hand came over to see me and I recited to him the Proclamation from the Easter Rising.'

Seamus McDonagh, Ireland's goalkeeper in the 1980s, quoted in Paul Rowan, *The Team That Jack Built* (1994).

'At no tyme to use ne occupye ye hurlinge of ye litill balle with the hookie stickies or staves, nor use no hand balle to play without the walls, but only the great foote balle.'

Archives of the Town of Galway (1527).

Headlines and Headline Writers

Ireland has a tenuous connection with the most famous soccer newspaper headline of them all – Paul Hickon's classic 'Super Caley Go Ballistic, Celtic Are Atrocious' in *The Sun* on 9 February 2000 after Caledonian Thistle defeated Glasgow Celtic 3–1 in the Scottish Cup. Subeditors everywhere have to rise to the challenge to find a better one.

'Ruud of the Red Goals Reigns Here.'
Sunday World headline by Eamonn Gibson after Ruud Van Nistelrooy scored for Manchester United the week before Christmas.

'Harps in Nine-Goal Thriller.'
Donegal Democrat headline after Finn Harps lost 7–2.

'Irish frivolity masks both fitness and resolve.'
The Times headline (1982).

'Jackson Stops McCabe.'
Irish Independent headline after a penalty save by the St Pat's goalkeeper.

'The Saint Versus the Sinner.'
Report of punch-up involving Lawrie McMenemy when he was at Southampton and England player Mark Wright.

'Turkey get roasted in Dalymount Cauldron.'
Irish Press headline after the Ireland v. Turkey match (1975).

'Golden Jason Fleece Dutch.'
Sunday Tribune headline describing that match (2001).

'Olé, Ól é.'
Spanish–Irish multilingual pun in an *Irish Independent* piece about the Submarine Bar.

'Oh God, That Was So Stupid.'
Translation of headline in German newspaper *Die Bild* after Germany conceded a late goal to Ireland during the 2002 World Cup finals.

'Sleepless in Seoul.'
The party that kept the Irish team awake during the 2002 World Cup inspired similar headlines in many newspapers.

'Suwonsong.'

Irish Examiner headline after Ireland's exit from the 2002 World Cup finals.

'Don Givens 4 Turkey 0.'

Turkish newspaper headline after a match at Dalymount (1975).

'We had no picture of Socrates so here is a picture of Plato instead.'

Arthur Mathews, caption in *Hot Press*' World Cup preview (1982).

'I know you lot don't write the headlines. But I'd like to meet the twit that does.'

Mick McCarthy (December 2005).

'The only Irish international who doesn't know where Dublin is.'

Manchester Evening News, after Shay Given failed to see Dion Dublin sneaking him to snatch the ball from him and score.

'My Left Foot.'

Irish Press, on night after Kevin Sheedy's goal earned Ireland a draw against England (1990).

Heroes

Every generation creates its heroes and elevates their deeds, they grow in stature even more when they have stopped playing. The greatest Irish players of all time may well have kicked the leather around in 1914, when technically we won the world championship. But it is more politically correct to select the ones who have brought Irish teams to six World Cup finals – three for the North and three for the South.

'I scored my first big-time goal and what a feeling I got – something I can never hope to describe. It seemed I would burst with happiness.'

Liam Whelan, casualty of the Munich air disaster.

'I think that record is like a weight around my neck right now and I wish Don Givens had scored fifty and everyone would leave me alone.'

Niall Quinn, speaking as he closed in on Givens' record.

'"The prostrate body of Ireland's two-goal hero was being ferried over the heads of a sea of supporters on the dance floor, on a conveyor belt of hands. Can you imagine that happening in any other country?" Andy observed. He was right. In England they'd have thumped him.'

Tony Cascarino, *Full Time: The Secret Life of Tony Cascarino* (2000).

'He is that rare Irishman, he made the most of his gifts.'

Con Houlihan, on Liam Brady, *Evening Press*.

'I wanted to use his ability on the edge of their 18-year box, not on the edge of ours.'

Jack Charlton, on Liam Brady.

'With Ireland they don't give up their f–king heroes easily, so you have got to show them.'

Jack Charlton, quoted in Paul Rowan, *The Team That Jack Built* (1994).

'Playing Stanley Matthews is like playing a ghost.'

Johnny Carey.

'He did it on purpose'

Peter Collins, explaining Gary Breen's toe-poke goal against Saudi Arabia during the 2002 World Cup finals.

'I'm just one of the players who got the ball for better players to play with.'

Tony Dunne.

'I see he kept a clean sheet again.'

Joke when John Aldridge was waiting to score his first goal
for Ireland.

'I don't have a girlfriend at the moment. I'm engaged to Inter
Milan.'

Robbie Keane (2000).

'When I was a kid I always watched Italian football on TV.
Playing in the back streets of Dublin I always pretended I was
playing for Inter.'

Robbie Keane, on signing for Internazionale (2000).

'Phil Babb is the guy with the most lusted after legs in English
football.'

Lisa l'Anson, compere of TV show *Dear Dilemma 1999*
(2000).

'I remember a Saturday when Arsenal fielded seven players
from this small island. Of course you can name them – Pat
Jennings, Pat Rice, John Devine, Sammy Nelson, David
O'Leary, Liam Brady and Frank Stapleton.'

Con Houlihan, *Evening Press*.

'Funny how the misses are as memorable as the goals. In the
qualifiers for the 1992 European Championship, I missed a
sitter against England in Wembley with two minutes to go.
Jack Charlton had a go at me when I came back in saying –
you could have been a hero twice over.'

Ray Houghton.

'At QPR, I am the target man. That's why I love having Ray Treacy with me. He becomes the target man.'

Don Givens, speaking after he scored four goals against Turkey in the qualifiers for the 1976 European Championship.

'Who's that standing beside Charlie Tully?'

Punchline of a 1940s joke about a visit to Vatican by the Celtic player and Irish international.

'When you spoke to Shay Given he looked in your eyes. He took in everything you had to say.'

Packie Bonner.

'The German government has been sending me to Highbury to study football technique but they should have sent me to Dublin to watch Paddy Moore.'

Dr Otto Nertz, German coach, after Ireland beat Germany 5-2 in Dalymount Park (1936).

'Dad told me that he had once seen the great Dixie Dean playing for Sligo against Dundalk. The way Dad remembered it, Dean had done nothing for eighty-five minutes of the match. With Sligo a goal down and no sign of anything special from Dixie, the crowd had decided that he was a has-been. People had been heading for exits when he had come to life. In the last few minutes, Dixie had moved twice. Wham, bang, two goals went in – Sligo won 2–1. It just went to show that you had to hang in there until the end if you wanted to succeed.'

Ferdia Mac Anna, *The Rocky Years* (2006).

'No one was more surprised than Sligo Rovers when the player with a goal in every hod of his head retracted.'
Report in *Sligo Champion* (28 January 1939). The newspaper reported that a crowd of 600 came to Sligo station to see Dixie Dean's arrival, despite earlier reports he had turned down an approach to join Sligo Rovers. He played for the club for five months and helped Sligo reach the 1939 FAI Cup final.

'Someone should tell the Shelbourne lads they are not expected to win.'
Comment by fan attending Dixie Dean's debut Sligo Rovers v. Shelbourne, *Sligo Champion* (4 February 1939).

'The pass-back changed everything. I would love to have been allowed come out of the goal.'
Packie Bonner.

'I'm going stagnant in the shop.'
Raich Carter, former English international, announcing he was coming out of retirement at 39 to play for Cork Athletic in 1953. Quoted in Dave Galvin and Gerry Desmond, *Irish Football Handbook*.

'A player like him could never be at his best on a pitch like that. But we'd still give him the ball and the crowd would go mad.'
Bertie O'Sullivan of Cork Celtic, on George Best's first appearances for the club after he signed in December 1975. Best was among a group of celebrity footballers – including Rodney Marsh (Drogheda), Terry Venables and Gordon

Banks (St Patrick's Athletic) and Bobby Charlton (Waterford)
– who made brief appearances for League of Ireland clubs.

'It beats me why people are deciding to retire from international football. I learned I had retired from international
football when my name wasn't on the list.'

Ray Treacy.

'I'd been brought up on Gaelic football. Crosses into the box,
were a problem for most goalkeepers, were ten a penny for
me.'

Pat Jennings.

'We're all remembered as better players now than we were
when we were playing. I was enthusiastic but limited in
ability.'

Noel Cantwell, quoted in Colm Keane, *Ireland's Soccer Top
Twenty* (2004).

'Elisha Scott once met Dixie Dean in the street. Dean nodded
to say hello and Scott dived full length to save the non-
existent header.'

Quoted in Francis Hodgson, *Only the Goalkeeper to Beat*
(1998). Scott was one of Ireland's greatest goalkeepers.

Historic Moments and Historic Days

We don't tend to see ourselves as a successful soccer-playing nation, but Irish teams have reached the quarter-finals of the Olympics when it was the premier soccer competition (1924), the quarter-finals of the World Cup (1958 and 1990), reached the second phase of the World Cup finals (1982, 1994 and 2002), qualified for the World Cup finals (1986), reached the European Championship quarter-finals (1964 and 1988), the semi-finals of the World Youth Cup (1984 and 1997) and won European Under-16 and Under-18 titles (1998). And there have been countless other acts of heroism along the way.

Goodison, 1949: Ireland 2 England 0

'There was a magician's convention in the hotel we stayed in Southport and I kept thinking we would need a magician to beat England.'

Con Martin.

'A cute lob, all the papers called it, but I'm not going to pretend it was. I just closed my eyes and banged it.'

Peter Farrell, talking about Ireland's second goal in Goodison.

'England's team had their fancy pants well and truly dusted by the wholehearted Éire men. Clancy certainly lowered the boom in a big way to humiliate England.'

Frank Butler, *Daily Express*.

'Football history, bleak black history was made. Let it be known that this was the first time that any country outside of the international championship has won here. Éire, small and weak by soccer standards, triumphed where the great European teams in their pre-war hey-days always failed. Before the gloom is too deep upon me, all praise to the boys in green, brilliantly skippered and set in a good example by right-back Johnny Carey they caught England fuddling and fiddling like a junior girls' hockey side, set about them with keen swift direct action, and flayed the hides off them.'

Clifford Webb, *Daily Herald*.

'No one among the 50,000 onlookers grudged the Irishmen their great win, though the result could easily have gone the other way. By keeping the ball close the forwards played into the hands of John Carey, Ireland's great right-back and captain, for whom today's result was a crowning triumph.'

Frank Coles, *Daily Telegraph.*

'England's soccer pride was humbled when the unfancied Éire team caused football's most surprising result for many years. It was a day of triumph for the Irish side.'

John Thompson, *Daily Mirror.*

'The impossible happened when the Éire team that was not expected to have a 100/1 chance humbled England.'

Jack Milligan, *Daily Graphic.*

'Eleven gallant men from Éire humbled England's soccer pride unmistakably. The Irish backs played wide out on the flanks while the rest of the defence massed in the penalty area. England's forwards had no answer to the plan.'

Charles Buchan, *News Chronicle.*

'This was the most fantastic international result of all time. Tommy Godwin brilliantly thought he played and positioned himself, there were times when it seemed that the carpenter had boarded up his goal.'

Roy Peskett, *Daily Mail.*

'Éire won a remarkable victory. Those who gently whispered something about the proverbial luck of the Irish will only have hit upon a fraction of the truth for the Éire goal did at times seem to bear a charmed life in the later stages of the afternoon. The solid fact remains that the England forwards had the ball at their command for four-fifths of the second half and yet could not turn their position to account. This indeed was a great day for the Irish and they gained a victory they will long remember.'

The Times.

'The British lion was in a sorry state last night. His den had been invaded and his tail had been twisted by the FAI soccer eleven, who scored a sensational 2–0 win.'

W. P. Murphy, *Irish Independent.*

Wembley, 1957: England 5 Ireland 1

'It was almost like a home match for the Irishmen. Most of the 52,000 crowd, Wembley was half-empty for the first tax-free game, were solid behind the players in green shirts. The cheers for their efforts and the occasional barracking of English stars did not spur the visitors to great effort.'

The Sporting Life.

'This score in fact did scant justice to the clever approach work of an Irish side so full of fire and enthusiasm that for long periods of the second half they had England looking jaded and scrambling their way untidily out of defence.'

The Times.

Dalymount, 1957: Ireland 1 England 1

'Ireland were denied victory by the width of my lace. The ball hit the lace of my boot and lifted over the heads of Charlie Hurley and Tommy Taylor and it went to Atyeo, the

big player with the brown boots and probably the worst player on the park and he was on his own to head the equaliser.'
Noel Cantwell.

'The silence after Atyeo's goal could be heard at Nelson's pillar.'
Irish Press.

'The hush was deafening.'
Colm Keane of RTÉ, introducing a radio archive recording to the reaction to John Atyeo's goal.

'England this was robbery. We stole away from Dalymount with our reputation in tatters and the spirit deadened by the thunderous roar of the Irish. For England, with startling luck, had escaped the consequence of a thoroughly shabby performance.'
The Daily Sketch.

'One of the most stirring internationals Ireland have taken part in since the war. A good ration of clever football not only for England but also from the Irishmen. Everyone had something in his hand, perhaps even a shillelagh. The entire ground was a picture of waving handkerchiefs and green and orange banners. The roar of encouragement was deafening as the seconds ticked closer to an Irish victory over the ancient foe. Then came the twist at the end. The next second Dalymount Park was as flat as a pricked balloon and as silent as the grave. If an anti-climax can be effective, this was it.'
The Times.

'It was daylight robbery at Dalymount Park. 47,000 indignant Irishmen went home wondering how England managed to grab a draw. This was one of the bitterest blows Éire's footballers have ever had to suffer. A goal up in four minutes they out-played, out-stayed and at time out-classed this shabby England. I shall never forget that moment Dalymount Park had echoed and re-echoed to the thunderous roar of the crowd cheering their side to victory.'

The News Chronicle.

'Oh the sadness of it all. Keening lament rose into the bright blue skies for the Irish had suddenly remembered all their old sorrow. They had whipped this pathetic collection that had been labelled England. Licked them for spirit and outclassed them for skill. They had tamed the England forward line and reduced the defence to panicked desperate fumblers.'

Daily Express.

'Forget the luck of the Irish after this undeserved equaliser. John Atyeo's header from Finney's centre was scored in a stupefied silence cutting abruptly short the victory roar which had been swelling across Dalymount Park for several minutes.'

Daily Mail.

'That goal turned a golden day of glory in Stygian darkness for the crestfallen Irish, never has a score been received in stonier silence and never has a draw tasted so like defeat. For though Ireland got a point from yesterday's game two were needed.'

W. P. Murphy, *Irish Independent.*

World Cup finals, 1958

'Do you know, we went to the World Cup with only 17 players. We hadn't any more of the necessary quality. In our quarter-final match against France, we had three players injured and we had to play with our reserve players. We came back and I remember on a bus around Belfast City Hall everybody was cheering and saying what a good team it was.'

Billy Bingham.

'It was an achievement to qualify for the final series and the more remarkable that we would finish in the top eight. We played against terrific odds that lengthened with every injury which hit us. No country in the history of world soccer earned as much glory in ultimate defeat as we did.'

Peter Doherty, on Northern Ireland's World Cup quarter-final appearance.

'We did not win anything. But as the Cinderellas of the soccer world, we made quite a stir at the ball.'

Danny Blanchflower, on Northern Ireland's World Cup quarter-final appearance.

Dalymount, 1959: Ireland 3 Sweden 2

'The best football an Irish team played at Dalymount Park.'
Johnny Carey.

'There is still 80 minutes to go.'

Noel Cantwell, speaking to Charlie Hurley after ten minutes when Sweden were 2-0 up.

'It was not my foot, it was my shadow.'

Simonsson, speaking after the game on why he did not play well.

'The bunch of imps who met for the first time at lunch yesterday, put on Irish jerseys, and went out and beat the super Swedes.'

Daily Mail.

'Suddenly, from nowhere, you're in the dressing room getting ready for the match beside your heroes.'

John Giles, on his selection for the Irish team, quoted in Colm Keane, *Ireland's Soccer Top Twenty* (2004).

Dalymount, 1963 Ireland 3 Austria 2

'It was fabulous, fighting back from a goal down with ten fit men to be one in front when they slid in the equaliser. Then in the last minute, as we thought, we get this wonderful gift of a penalty and victory and out on the field rush these too enthusiastic Irish supporters to wreck our hopes.'

Charlie Hurley.

Dalymount, 1965: Ireland 1 Spain 0

'I shouted at Iribar when I realised I wasn't going to get the ball. I don't know what I shouted at him, I just wanted to put a bit of fear in him. He put the ball in the net and afterwards called me an animal even though I didn't get near him.'

Noel Cantwell, on Ireland's surprise 1-0 win over Spain in the 1966 World Cup qualifiers.

'Loco the man's mad, he's a bull and he's mad.'

Iribar, quoted after the game, quoted in Colm Keane, *Ireland's Soccer Top Twenty* (2004).

Prague, 1967: Czechoslovakia 1 Ireland 2

'Popluhar was one of the best players in Europe and he had this magnificent trick of turning and sending the ball past people. I was knackered from chasing him all night and couldn't keep up with him so when he did his shimmy and sent the ball around the place I should have been he bounced it off me instead. The ball bounced over to Turlough O'Connor and he scored the winning goal. Popluhar was amazed at how I had read exactly what he was going to do. I grinned at him and didn't tell him the truth.'

Ray Treacy, speaking on how bottom-placed Ireland got the winning goal to beat top-placed Czechoslovakia 2-1 in a European qualifier in Prague. Treacy had headed home Ireland's first goal. Ireland didn't win another match for five years.

Dalymount, 1974: Ireland 3 Soviet Union 0

'An awful lot of people seem to have been at Dalymount that day. Everybody I have met since was at the game.'
Don Givens, on his three goals against the Soviet Union.

World Cup finals, 1982

'I watched their little knees and some of them were trembling.'
Billy Bingham, talking after Northern Ireland's match against Spain in Valencia, when Northern Ireland won 1-0, thanks to a Gerry Armstrong goal, despite being reduced to ten men.

'For God's sake don't breathe on any of the Spanish players in the penalty box. Don't even breathe on them or they'll give a penalty kick. Be very careful.'
Billy Bingham.

'If you go over the halfway line I'll kick you up the backside.'
Billy Bingham, instructing Sammy Nelson.

'Here we were in the Spanish bullring and we slew the bull.'
Billy Bingham.

'I saw that the ball was too high for Juanito to reach, and I sensed if I made contact with him I might be penalised and the game might slip from our grasp. So I knew exactly what I was doing when I tipped the ball over his head and dived to retrieve it. Later I was told that millions of viewers in Ireland had their hearts of their mouths at that instant. I can only repeat that, however it looked, I had the situation under control.'

Pat Jennings, on the injury-time save against Spain, *An Autobiography* (1983).

Lansdowne Road, 1984: Ireland 1 Soviet Union 0

'The most agonising countdown in Irish football since the night John Atyeo's equaliser earned an improbable reprieve for England.'

Peter Byrne.

Lansdowne Road, 2001: Ireland 1 Netherlands 0

'Every game has a turning point and this undoubtedly was the one. Ireland were down to ten men, Holland added Hasselbank and Van Hooijdonk to their already considerable strike force and I don't believe anyone in the ground would have expected Ireland to hold on for a draw. For thirty minutes we expected it would be backs-to-the-wall for Ireland, and for ten minutes it was until, incredibly, and against all the odds, Jason McAteer scored.'

Tony Cascarino.

Injuries

The worst word in the soccer lexicon. No wonder they make such a laugh about it.

'Kevin Moran never hesitates to put his head where most players would hesitate to put their boot.'
Breandán Ó hEithir.

'Jamie Carragher looks like he's got cramp in both groins.'
Andy Townsend (May 2005).

'Achilles tendon injuries are a pain in the butt.'
Dave O'Leary.

'He's got a knock on his shin there, just above the knee.'
Frank Stapleton

'Mick McCarthy will have to replace Cascarino because he's quickly running out of legs.'

Mark Lawrenson.

'Last year I had a foot operation. Then in my first game my thigh went in the warm up. This season I'm going to play it by ear.'

John Aldridge (1995).

'I didn't like kicking or being kicked.'

Oscar Wilde, on being asked if he had played football at school.

'If he has admitted he went out to do him, he hasn't a leg to stand on.'

Ally McCoist, on the Roy Keane–Alf-Inge Haaland affair.

'In years gone by Arsenal have kicked themselves in the foot many times.'

John Aldridge.

'To bring down one man is good but three, that must be a record.'

Tom Tyrrell.

'Its like someone walking down the street and there's a big block of wood. If you don't see it you are going to walk into it and fall over.'

John Giles, on players who go down too easily when they are tackled.

'The crazy thing about throwing things is you can hit your own players. Though you shouldn't be throwing things at all.'
Tom Tyrrell.

'His face is such a mess I'm going to bring him home and put him on the mantelpiece to keep the kids away from the fire.'
Dermot Keeley, talking about a League of Ireland player.

'When Neil [Lennon] played for me, he ran his legs off.'
Lawrie McMenemy.

'I think he's caught him. It is like a punch you would get off your rabbit.'
Damien Richardson.

Italia '90

Ireland first accepted, then turned down an invitation to travel to the World Cup finals of 1950 on the grounds that the players were on holidays and the trip would cost too much. Forty years later, qualifying for the finals, a near thing in 1974 and 1982, had become an obsession. So when Ireland eventually did qualify in 1990 and got to the quarter-final stage, the country partied with the sort of abandon that ensured everybody on the island was caught up in it, whether they had any interest in soccer or not.

'After Packie had saved and David had scored, we were back in the Hotel Bristol. The night was surprisingly quiet, unlike the crazy aftermath of our victory over England in Stuttgart.'
Con Houlihan.

'It is up to the manager and staff to relieve boredom, to make sure we have enough videos and games. In 1990 we didn't have any. None. No videos, no games like Trivial Pursuits. All we could do was watch football videos and Italian TV. We all watched a programme called *Tutti Frutti*. I still haven't a clue what it was about. All you had to cool you off was this fan that made a terrible racket when it was turned on. That left you with three options: open the window and let in the mosquitoes, leave the fan off and sweat, or turn the fan on, put up with the racket and watch it going round and round for as long as you could stand it before switching it off and going to sleep.'

Ray Houghton.

'On that hot summer afternoon in June there was no greater celebrity than to play for the team that Jack built. We were masters of the universe. Kings.'

Tony Cascarino, *Full Time: The Secret Life of Tony Cascarino* (2000).

'Jack Charlton met Bobby Robson walking down the street. Bobby Robson was carrying a television.

Jack: "What's that for?"

Bobby: "I got it for the players."

Jack: "I suppose that's a fair swap."'

Joke from Italia '90.

'Mick McCarthy arrived in the dressing room at half-time with a badly bruised leg. They're still trying to figure out whose it was.'

Joke from Italia '90.

'A 1–1 draw with the Republic of Ireland that was portrayed, by *The Sun* in particular, as just about the end of English civilisation.'

Bobby Robson, *Farewell But Not Goodbye* (2005).

'Shame fills the heart of every right-thinking Englishman. How could our lads play like that? How could they let us down so badly?'

Editorial in *The Sun* after Ireland v. England (1990).

'It was unnatural for Mick to come back and look for the ball but he kept doing it. He did it a few times and the camera didn't catch me. But this time he did and I was shouting at him, and I kicked it in such a rage it went ten yards further.'

Packie Bonner, on his magical kickout that led to the equalising goal against England at the 1990 World Cup finals.

'The Irish sides that reached Euro '88, Italia '90 and the rest had no Thierry Henry. What we had was spirited, sometimes raw Irish talent and all the video analysis in the world won't give you that.'

Niall Quinn.

'I have the hardest working midfield in the entire competition.'

Jack Charlton.

'Olé, olé, olé, Sheedy saves the day.'

T-shirt slogan.

'If Bobby wants to play silly buggers so can I.'

Jack Charlton, on Bobby Robson's decision not to announce the England team until just before kick off.

'The way Ireland play forces you to play badly. No team manages to escape their contagious crap.'

Ahmed El-Mokadem, Egyptian sponsor.

'They never in ninety minutes threatened our game. They had one shot from thirty yards and I think they had a corner kick. They just sat back, closed it down, defended and we needed a break and didn't get it. One goal would have meant we were terrific, we didn't get the goal.'

Jack Charlton.

'I always felt that, if I got one chance, I would take it. Cascarino and I both knew he could send it somewhere near our direction so he took one side I took the other. It came down his side I thought I'll keep running here, and Van Breukelen dropped the ball and I thought, "My God, I might score." I can remember clearly going up to the ball, I knew I had a great chance, and I thought, "Don't miss, you can never go home if you miss", and I saw it hit the net and Ray Houghton landed on my back.'

Niall Quinn.

Referee: 'Play football.'

Mick McCarthy: 'We haven't played as much football ever before.'

Exchange during kick around winding down the Ireland–Netherlands match.

'No matter what happens, we've had a great time, we've enjoyed it.'
Jack Charlton, speaking before the penalty shootout against Romania.

'I don't think you should place them, I think you should bash them. Then you are going to take a penalty, make your mind up and do whatever you have decided. Don't change your mind. Put it down, do what you think best.'
Jack Charlton, advising players before the penalties were taken.

'All the best. And don't change your mind. If you miss, you miss.'
Kevin Sheedy, advising Dave O'Leary before his last penalty.

'Missing never crossed my mind. It was so quick. You had to get the ball down and get down there.'
Dave O'Leary.

'Schillaci, 6'2", eyes of blue, Mick McCarthy's after you, la la la la la la la la la la.'
Irish supporters' song.

'Schillaci, 6'2", black and blue, Mick McCarthy's after you, la la.
Irish supporters' song, second verse.

'Tony Cascarino, won't be on the vino, la, la, la.'
Irish supporters' song.

'They played this dreadful dirge about lowering somebody or other into the ground on the team bus.'

Jack Charlton, speaking before the quarter-final against Italy.

'I didn't want to do a press call. I just wanted a drink with the lads, and get away back to the hotel. Then somebody said: "They want you out on the ground." I said, "We'll all come out in a minute when I get them together." But they said, "They want you out because the crowd won't go until you go out." Myself and Maurice walked out into the stadium. There was nearly as many green and white as there was during the game. They just sang and enjoyed the occasion. I'm sure that memory will live in the minds of all the Irish who were there. It was like we had won. They weren't acting like we got beat, they weren't steaming with their heads down and looking miserable. They were waving and singing, and someone had given me a flag, and they all waved our flags and we waved our flags. I don't get emotional very often, but I got emotional then.'

Jack Charlton.

'Jack Charlton has made a lot from a little.'

L'Equipe, the French sports newspaper.

'We may not have won the World Cup but I like to think that in a real sense all of us, players, officials and supporters, restored some of the old, decent values to the game. And in so doing, we may, perhaps have left our mark on the development of football in the years ahead.'

Jack Charlton.

'A publican called me in to his premises and said to me, "You see this room. During the World Cup it was heaving with people, we had three or four hundred people in here. We had a big screen at that end and another at that end." And he got a bottle of the best brandy in a big white box and he said, "I want to give you this. This is your share of the profits."'

Jack Charlton.

'I think the goalkeeper went for the sod of grass Cas kicked as the ball bobbled in under him.'

Mick McCarthy, on Cascarino's penalty during the shootout at Genoa.

'I always felt I'd love to test myself to see if I could put myself in that position. It fell to me. I knew I was up to it but I had to go and prove it.'

Dave O'Leary, on the penalty against Romania in Genoa.

'We've qualified for the World Cup. Let's go out and compete.'

Jack Charlton, talking about his philosophy, as incorporated in the team-song for Italia '90.

'I went out to the garden and my son came running out to tell me that Dave had taken a penalty and Ireland had won. I said don't be silly, daddy doesn't take penalties.'

Dave O'Leary's wife, Joy, famously disinterested in soccer, who managed to miss all the excitement.

'Anyone who sends a team out like that should be ashamed of themselves. We know about the upside of Jack. We know how hard these lads work. We know about their courage. But football is a two sided game. I feel embarrassed for soccer, embarrassed for the country, embarrassed for all the good players, for our great tradition in soccer. This is nothing to do with the players who played today. That's a good side. I feel embarrassed and ashamed of that performance, and we should be.'

Eamon Dunphy after Ireland's 0-0 draw with Egypt. He finished by throwing a pen and thus began the 'ashamed to be Irish' legend.

'I wasn't keen on it at all. Centre-backs taking penalties, that's a no no. I was delighted the goalkeeper went the wrong way.'

Jack Charlton.

'Football was the excuse for a lot of good behaviour. If David O'Leary could forgive Jack Charlton, who could not be reconciled? Neighbours who hadn't talked to each other in years embraced and pledged undying affection in alcohol-infused tears. If the sun felt hotter in those summers it was because there was so much human warmth in the air.'

Fintan O'Toole (2001).

Jack Charlton:
The Jack Who Would Be King

Nobody has yet defined what Charlton's motivating force as Irish manager was – a sense of mischievous fun, genuine affection for the culture he recognised as close to that of his Geordie youth, the settling of old scores with the English FA, or sheer bloody-mindedness? He stuck the job for ten years, which may be longer than any manager will again.

'Jack is not always right, but he is never wrong.'
John Giles.

'Jack understood that your team was your family, and you didn't expose your family and expect to retain their respect.'
Tony Cascarino, *Full Time: The Secret Life of Tony Cascarino* (2000).

'I have always believed that had Alan McLoughlin not equalised with a volley from the edge of the box there's a fair chance Jack would have chinned me.'

Tony Cascarino, retelling how he left his jersey in the dressing room at Windsor Park in 1993, as related in *Full Time: The Secret Life of Tony Cascarino* (2000).

'Jack only says that because we lost.'

Mick Byrne, on Jack Charlton's story that he allowed Mick to pick the team for the match against Wales in 1986.

'If Jack came in here now he wouldn't buy a drink. He'd be hoping someone else would buy one.'

Roy Keane.

'Jack Charlton developed a style of play that suite his crude convictions rather than the gifts of his players.'

Roy Keane.

'The honour that pleased me most was when I was voted Beer Drinker of the Year.'

Jack Charlton.

'I have a little black book with the names of two players in it, and if I get the chance to do them I will. I'll make them suffer before I pack the game in. If I can kick them four yards over the touchline, believe me, I will.'

The original famous Jack Charlton quotation.

'Soccer is a man' game, not an outing for namby-pambies.'

Jack Charlton.

'We are on the crest of a slump.'

Jack Charlton, speaking a few days before resigning as Middlesbrough manager.

'The final indignity came when our team coach got stuck in the mud when we tried to leave the bloody place. In vain, twenty strong men tried to shift it, and we were forced to stand there, red-faced, until a replacement coach arrived.'

Jack Charlton, speaking on Sheffield Wednesday's 1977 defeat at non-league Wigan Athletic, in his autobiography, *Jack Charlton* (1996).

'Managing Ireland is really a part-time job. All international team managers are part-time.'

Jack Charlton.

'I'm very placid most of the time but I blow up very quickly. I shout and I wave my arms, my lip twitches, I become incoherent and I swear. All at the same time.'

Jack Charlton (1973).

I'm too outspoken and I disagree with too much in football at the moment. I disagree with the way managers are treated. I disagree with the way their clubs are treated. I think I've got too many strong views to become England manager.'

Jack Charlton.

'If it was a toss-up between making a winning tackle and landing a big fish, I think the fish wins every time.'

Jack Charlton.

'George Best used to say that I couldn't play. My answer to that was that I knew enough to stop buggers like him playing.'

Jack Charlton.

'I learned there was more to life than working seven days a week in football and driving endless hours at night on the motorways to watch matches. I realised I had missed seeing my children growing up.'

Jack Charlton.

'I'm a football player.'

'And I'm Doris Day.'

Jack Charlton, recounting his first conversation with his wife.

'The fans very rarely get to the managers. The press get to them. The press start saying the manager is under pressure. They tell the directors the manager is under pressure before the directors have even thought of it.'

Jack Charlton (1991).

'It is their decision, not the press or the media. The people in Ireland. I am pretty sensitive to the feelings of people, and I feel that I will know the moment they decide they would like a change. When that happens I will give it to them.'

Jack Charlton.

'I can't swear on television. I don't swear on front of women and I don't swear on front of children. On the odd occasion when I am expressing a view or making a point, I do use an expletive just to strengthen the sentence. But I don't expect to be quoted by every journalist every time I use a four-letter word in whatever sense or whatever.'

Jack Charlton, speaking on *The Late Late Show* (1994).

'You go into a pub and they used to have pictures of John F. Kennedy or the Pope on the walls. Now it's Jack everywhere.'

Niall Quinn, on Charlton's retirement (1995).

'I would not pick anyone from the League of Ireland unless I thought they were capable of handling it and we have never really come across any, with the exception of one, Pat Byrne.'

Jack Charlton.

'I think not only will I be remembered by the Irish for the ten years but I'm also remembered, strangely enough, by the English people for those ten years, because the English public followed the Irish in a way they had never done before.'

Jack Charlton, quoted in Colm Keane, *A Cut Above the Rest* (1998).

'I was disappointed in them. I don't know what it is. Maybe it is because you like people to try to talk you out of it.'

Jack Charlton, speaking on his resignation, quoted in Colm Keane, *A Cut Above the Rest* (1998).

'I phoned Dave [O'Leary] and said, "Are you coming?" And he said, "No I'm going on holiday." And I said, "Well it's a bit more important than your holidays. Cancel your holidays, you can take them any bloody time." And he said, "Ah no, the arrangements have been made." And I said, "Okay then, forget it." Now, David wasn't going to come back to us for three years but that wasn't my fault.'

Charlton, quoted in Paul Rowan, *The Team That Jack Built* (1994).

'The major difference between Jack Charlton and Daniel O'Connell is that he survived Genoa.'

The Leader, commenting on a proposal in 1996 to build a monument to Jack Charlton in O'Connell Street.

'Thanks, Jack, you have been a manager in a million.'

Louis Kilcoyne, FAI President.

'It is not overstating the case that the FAI now finds itself with a manager it does not want.'

Peter Byrne, after Jack Charlton's appointment as Irish team manager, *The Irish Times* (1986).

'Jack Charlton talks a good game. Yesterday he produced a stinker and in a decent country the spectators would be entitled to a refund. I am tempted to sell off my property in Spain and the Canaries and give the proceeds to the FAI. Then they could pay off the manager who should never have been appointed.'

Con Houlihan, after Charlton's first game in charge of Ireland, *Evening Press*.

'If we get to England for the European Championship finals in 1996 we'll have bigger gates than them. Oh I'd bloody love that.'

Jack Charlton (1994).

'I'm always suspicious of games when you are the only ones who play it.'

Jack Charlton, on hurling (1988).

'I wasn't sure it was Jack at first. But then I saw his hair flapping in the breeze. No one has hair that flaps in the breeze the way Jack's does.'

Brian O'Byrne, Irish fan, who ran on to the field after the Ireland–Italy match and on whose behalf Jack Charlton intervened with the security staff.

'Jack Charlton makes out that he's not really interested in football, and tells the whole world he has gone fishing. But we know what he is thinking about when he's fishing. Football.'

Johann Cruyff, on Jack Charlton (1990).

Japan and Korea 2002:
Two Countries, One Dilemma

Ireland went out of the 2002 World Cup finals on penalties having reached the last sixteen of what was, in many ways, the most interesting of the tournaments. While Saipan deserves a separate section of its own, Ireland's performance will be recognised as an achievement in the face of considerable adversity and the end, rather than the beginning, of a great adventure.

'We are the team that doesn't study the opposition, that takes supporters on the team coach, is not really bothered, that likes the pint and the crack. And yet here we are in the last sixteen of the World Cup again. If that scenario were true we must be the greatest group of guys that ever played the game.

Mick McCarthy.

'The history of the Republic's football is specked with gallant defeats. This was a gallant draw.'
Con Houlihan, *Sunday World*.

'Everyone has been telling us all week what a big game it was. You want to try sitting in that dug-out when your backside's in the bacon slicer!'
Mick McCarthy, talking after Ireland's 3–0 win over Saudi Arabia.

'I had to drink eight bottles of water before I could produce. It worked but it didn't help me much that night in bed.'
Robbie Keane, on the problems he faced providing the necessary goods for a dope test following the match with Saudi Arabia.

'Imagine a kid in a sweet shop, who's just been given freedom of the premises. I saw that kid in Yokohama. His name was Damien Duff. He'd just scored, was running back to the halfway line and his face was frozen with the sweetest smile.'
Niall Quinn.

'There are no excuses. The penalties were just dreadful. I don't feel for the players who missed them at all.'
Jack Charlton, talking after Ireland's defeat on penalties to Spain.

'It's a no-win game for us, although I suppose we can win by winning.'
Gary Doherty.

'Is the Roy situation now a case of sour grapes and the Robbie situation a case of sauerkraut?'
Letter writer to *The Irish Times*, after Ireland's draw with Germany.

'We weren't lucky. It's the Irish who have a flower in their backsides – they got a penalty in the 89th minute, we had to play extra-time with nine and a half players, and the referee was unreal.'
Jose Antonio Camacho, Spain's manager, talking after the same game.

'I'm 35 years of age I thought I'd seen it all and I'd seen nothing.'
Niall Quinn.

'There was a lot of suffering.'
Iker Casillas, the Spanish goalkeeper.

'We gave a better performance in all four games than we did in our games in 1990 and certainly better than 1994. We are as good as any team in the tournament.'
Liam Brady.

'Ireland have got to score to win the game.'
Bobby Robson.

'There's late. Then there's fashionably late. Keane's goal was positively haute couture.'
Miriam Lord, *Irish Independent*.

'You can't go doing that. That's outrageous. That's rugby.'
Jim Beglin, talking as Niall Quinn was fouled against Spain.

'The public think we're a gobshite organisation, end of story.
Can you blame them?'
An FAI official, quoted in *The Sunday Times*.

'A little stud problem for Steve Finnan. It's been solved… by
a spanner.'
George Hamilton.

'I'm not going to shout out from the hotel window, "Oi, keep
the noise down."'
Mick McCarthy on Korea's celebrations.

'Given by name, given by nature.'
Joe Duffy, introducing Shay Given to the fans in the Phoenix
Park during the celebrations on the team's return.

'The goalkeeper Gay Shiven had a good game.'
Martin Dahlin, a Blackburn Rovers player, on Swedish TV.

'I'd hate to be waiting for a bus after all that.'
Bill O'Herlihy on the homecoming celebrations in the
Phoenix Park.

'The Irish World Cup journey ended as it began, with an FAI
official attempting to clarify the confusion surrounding Roy
Keane.'
Frank McNally, *The Irish Times*.

'I will be supporting Germany and Saudi Arabia in the contests ahead.'

Eamon Dunphy.

'Suwon. We'll add the name to the list of cities in which our hearts have ceased to beat and then started again with a shudder. Suwon. Gateway to Seoul, stairway to heaven. Suwon. A lank-haired blond called Mendietta scuffed a penalty kick past Shay Given and we heard the soft click of a door closing.'

Tom Humphries, *The Irish Times*.

'No regrets, none at all. My only regret is that we went out on penalties. That's my only regret. But no, no regrets.'

Mick McCarthy.

'The saddest day since the Battle of Kinsale – wasn't there a pre-match defection and a treacherous pundit there too?'

Evening Herald, after defeat to Spain.

Journalists:
The State of the Fourth Estate

In the old days, there were three of them, but now a cacophony of competing newspapers and broadcast media compete for the next big story. It is not journalism that has changed – just the size of it.

'I read the papers and they said we played badly last week. I thought we were fantastic, so it shows how much I know.'
David O'Leary (1999).

'The players were lucky. Their luggage came with them. There's nothing worse than arriving in a swanky hotel in a strange country without as much as a spare pair of knickers to call your own. And the few ladies on this trip were beginning to fret too.'
Miriam Lord, at the 2002 World Cup finals, *Irish Independent.*

'The ref gave a goal against us and as I turned around I saw this big furry microphone so I laid into it. I kicked it and it went spinning around like a boomerang and landed twenty yards away. Then the Sky touchline reporter came up to me and said, "So Mick, you must be disappointed."'

Mick McCarthy, talking about a game when he was the manager of Millwall.

'There is a simple recipe about this sports business. If you're a sporting star, you're a sporting star. If you don't quite make it, you become a coach. If you can't coach, you become a journalist. If you can't spell, you introduce *Grandstand* on a Saturday afternoon.'

Ennis-born Des Lynam, who introduced a BBC sports programme called, you've guessed it, *Grandstand*, on a Saturday afternoon.

'It's a lot of work this job. I got a phone call this morning from a journalist in India.'

Jack Charlton, during the 1994 World Cup finals.

'Can I go storming out now please?'

Jack Charlton, commenting on sensationalist coverage at press conference after Northern Ireland's match with the Republic.

'Theatre critics and film critics do know what the mechanics of a production are. Most football writers don't. So players tend to despise journalists. On the other hand, players are flattered by their attention. Flattered by the idea that this guy has come along specially to write about them.

So you have contempt and at the same time a slight awe at seeing your name in print.'
Eamon Dunphy, *Only a Game* (1976).

'If I'm in Ireland, I'll buy a few papers. I do a column for one of them but I can't remember its name.'
Jack Charlton (1994).

'One advantage of managing Northern Ireland and living in England is that you don't see the papers. They offered me some cuttings but I said no thanks.'
Lawrie McMenemy.

'They don't learn anything, they still attack the manager and players before a game.'
Mick McCarthy, talking about when he managed Ireland.

'Listen here, I've been to Olympics and European championships for years, and whenever did you ever hear of a journalist bringing a bomb into the press box?'
Peter O'Neill, unimpressed by another security check at the 1994 World Cup finals, *Sunday World*.

'Young Private Jumpy, with the authoritative Kalashnikov, wants to know what exactly we want. It seems like a silly question, but he's the one with the gun so he doesn't get a silly answer. We show him our beautiful, laminated accreditation dangler which identifies us as part of the World Cup family, or a distant ne'er-do-well cousin thereof. He is not impressed. He wants the letter. So we fish out the letter. It is a photocopy of a letter, actually, and it is on FAI notepaper with the FAI logo attached. Not exactly a symbol which prompts the response "that'll do nicely thank you" everywhere you travel. The letter is short and is written in Korean script. We have no idea what it says. It may say, "I am an Irish journalist. I mean no harm. Please don't shoot me."'

Tom Humphries, at the 2002 World Cup finals, *The Irish Times*.

'You're lucky, in your time you didn't have Joe Duffy interviewing you.'

Ray Houghton talking to John Giles, on RTÉ television during the homecoming from the 2002 World Cup finals.

'Some lad enters journalism and becomes a soccer reporter, immediately becomes a critic, and his views are now read and he considers them important.'

John Giles, quoted in Paul Rowan, *The Team That Jack Built* (1994).

'One of my colleagues will remember the trip to Bulgaria for a bizarre reason. When he went to put on his pyjamas all the buttons had been snipped off. That tells you something about the state of the Bulgarian economy.'

Con Houlihan.

'Shall I send Stan home and give you something to write about?'

Mick McCarthy, talking in the aftermath of Saipan.

Malcolm Brodie: 'Magnifico. Magnifico. Magnifico.'

Belfast Telegraph copytypist: 'It's okay, I heard you the first time.'

Legend of how the opening sentence of Ireland's veteran soccer writer's report of Northern Ireland's victory over Spain in 1982 almost didn't make it into the paper.

Keane-oh

The image of Roy Keane, Achilles-like, sulking before the gates of Troy inspired a musical full of togas and jokes about Cork. The debate about Roy Keane is greater than football.

'Sometimes, I think he thinks he's Alex Ferguson.'
Jason McAteer, on Keane's attitude.

'I'll have to see if any of Keane's studs are still in there.'
Alf-Inge Haaland, Manchester City midfielder, before a scan in his knee (2001).

'He was very, very drunk and as aggressive as you can imagine. He had evil in his eyes and he gave me a good kick. I still have the bruise.'
Leanne Carey, Australian tourist, after a wine bar assault by Keane (1999).

'I believe Lennox Lewis didn't see that punch coming and the skipper of the *Titanic* had some excuse for not spotting an iceberg in the dark. But I couldn't believe my big ears when Fergie said he had not seen Keane's tackle on Haaland and that United's secretary thought it was a sending off. A sending off? It was among the worst fouls I've ever seen.'
Brian Clough (2001).

'As if cutting Haaland in half was not enough, Keane then swoops on him like Dracula. All he needed was the black cloak.'
Brian Clough (2001).

'If I opened my mouth every time there was something wrong, I'd need my own newspaper.'
Roy Keane.

'I'm surprised he did a book in the first place. He'd be the first to give someone stick in the dressing room if they had done something similar.'
Denis Irwin.

'I made mistakes. I was naïve and probably drank too much.'
Roy Keane, *The Autobiography* (2002).

'I prefer the new Roy. He's calmed down a lot now. He's much easier – maybe he should have the other hip done.'
Paul Durkan, referee, on the all-new serene Mr Keane.

'I'm sick and tired of hearing commentators telling us how much running Keane does in a match, how he covers every blade of grass. He's entitled to be fresher than most because he has so much off-time, eight red cards and that long injury lay-off which was his fault. He's had more than enough rest through the suspensions alone.'

Brian Clough (2001).

'I'd rather buy a Bob the Builder CD for my two-year-old son.'

Jason McAteer, on buying Keane's autobiography (2002).

'It is tempting to regard Keane as the embodiment of the Celtic Tiger: ambitious, tired of being patted on the head, not wanting to settle for "heroic failure".'

Fintan O'Toole.

'His aura and presence – and those killer eyes – would command instant respect.'

Tony Cascarino.

'If I don't get stuck in I usually have a bad game. Work rate is a vital part of my game and I cannot change.'

Roy Keane (1995).

'John O'Shea was just strolling around when he should have been busting a gut to get back.'

Roy Keane, commenting on his team-mate as part of an interview that was deemed too strong for broadcast by Manchester United's official television channel.

'I like Nottingham. It's a bit like Ireland. My heart is with this club. My present contract has another year to go and I still have another one of three years in mind, but I now fancy something a bit longer.'

Roy Keane, denying, in January 1993, that he would leave Nottingham Forest if they were relegated. He left in July.

'I never thought I had anything interesting to say, but if I'm captain of Manchester United I must have, mustn't I?'

Roy Keane.

'I've got two dogs as well and I didn't fancy leaving them in quarantine for six months.'

Roy Keane, giving the real reason why he turned down offers to move to Spain and Italy (January 2000).

'I was in a shop last week buying a lottery ticket and someone asked, "Why are you going in for that?"'

Roy Keane, on life after signing a £52,000-a-week contract (January 2000).

'I came down to a restaurant and saw some of the lads sitting at a table eating sandwiches. I couldn't believe it. We'd discussed diet. F—king cheese sandwiches and hour and a half before training.'

Roy Keane.

'Before the game there was all this stuff about anti-racism and anti-bullying. It would be a good idea to start wearing wrist-bands for anti-diving.'

Roy Keane.

'You understand that not only is Roy very good, he's always very good. He knows that Keane is the better player but if you offered to make me a deal, to give me all the skill he has and the life he has to lead, I'd decline.'

Niall Quinn.

'I'd never put Keane in the real hard-man bracket, more the roll-up-your-sleeves leader every team wishes they had. He doesn't care who you are and what you've done in the game or in the last five minutes. If you're not pulling your weight, he'll bawl you out on front of 50,000 fans.'

Ian Wright, former Arsenal and England player.

'So, Roy Keane's on £50 grand a week? Mind you, I was on £50 grand a week until the police found my printing machine.'

Mickey Thomas, former soccer player, who spent time in jail for his part in a counterfeit currency scam.

'He earns fifty thousand quid, and he scores for Real Madrid.'

Arsenal fans, after Roy Keane put through his own goal in the same week as he negotiated a new contract.

'He shouldn't be elbowing my son in the head.'

Thora McAteer, mother of Jason, after his brush with Roy Keane.

'He was fannying. It was a PR stunt – again.'

Eamon Dunphy, on Niall Quinn's handshake with Keane after he was sent off.

'Uriah Rennie took some stick for stepping in between us, but I am thankful he did, because Roy would have ripped my head off.'

Jason McAteer.

'I was sent off for pushing him [Alan Shearer] – but if you're going to get sent off, you might as well punch him properly. It's the same punishment. You might as well get hung for a sheep as a lamb.'

Roy Keane.

'All of Lansdowne Road rose to greet him. Priests do not hand out forgiveness more freely.'

Amy Lawrence, journalist, on the return of Roy Keane to international soccer.

'Alfie was taking the piss. I'd waited long enough. I hit him hard. The ball was there (I think). Take that you c–t. And don't ever stand over me again sneering at fake injuries.'

Roy Keane, *The Autobiography* (2002).

'There is artistic licence.'

Eamon Dunphy, talking about the part in Keane's autobiography that deals with the notorious tackle on Alf-Inge Haaland.

'Hopefully I won't be sent off as captain. But if I was a betting man I wouldn't have much money on that.'

Roy Keane.

'I'd never change my game. It isn't possible. If I did I wouldn't be half the player I am. I'd be back in Irish football. I'll obviously be sent off a few more times. It's part and parcel of the game.'

Roy Keane.

'Ireland's spirit is because of Roy Keane's absence, not despite it.'

Letter to *The Irish Times*, during the 2002 World Cup finals.

'What probably unnerves most of us is the possibility that there might be a Roy Keane in our own lives – someone we trust implicitly, someone upon whom we depend totally, someone we have turned into an icon of personal responsibility and irreproachable loyalty; and who, when we need them most, will betray us; who, at the crunch, will be loyal to their own needs above our own.'

Kevin Myers, writing after the Saipan incident, *The Irish Times* (2002).

'Be bitter, Roy, otherwise you're going nowhere.'

Roy Keane, *The Autobiography* (2002).

'I get stick everywhere. Makes me feel at home.'

Roy Keane (1995).

'It is great to be on the pitch because that is when you feel the least pressure.'

Roy Keane.

'A lot of it might be fear, fear of failure, and not getting carried away with success.'
Roy Keane quoted by Colm Keane, *Ireland's Soccer Top Twenty* (2004).

'There's no difference between Roy Keane and any other player. The only thing is that he is a better player.'
Mick McCarthy.

'I only ever hit Roy the once. He got up again so I couldn't have hit him very hard.'
Brian Clough.

'He said to us all, "You go with the flow." I thought, "Here we go again." He'd been hammering me with the one-liners all week. I asked him, "What goes with the flow?" "Dead fish," he said. I thought, Wow, P-R-O-F-O-U-N-D, the Messiah has spoken.'
Jason McAteer (May 2002).

'The Roy Keane virus: Throws you out of windows.'
Internet joke (2001).

'Roy is inverted.'
John Aldridge (yes, he meant introverted).

'I don't think some of the people who come to Old Trafford can spell football, never mind understand it.'
Roy Keane.

Liam Tuohy

Ireland's last part-time manager, Liam Tuohy, tilled the ground for the soccer revival of the 1980s, brought a youth team to the World Cup semi-finals and was treated shamefully by Jack Charlton and the FAI for his pains.

'We'd go down and score this brilliant goal but I'd be having a go at somebody and fellows would say, "What the f—k is wrong with you, Rasher?" But that's he way I am. That's the way it gets you. And I think every football man is like that.'

Liam Tuohy, former Irish manager.

'I was married with five children and then Sheila had our sixth when I was at a game in Poland which didn't make me husband of the year.'

Liam Tuohy.

'There was a bit of glamour about Rovers. We'd travel to games in these Austin Princesses. And people used to say the green and white shirt made you look bigger. They'd see you afterwards and say, "Jaysus you're only a titch."'

Liam Tuohy, former Irish manager.

'We went in at half-time leading 1–0 but under serious pressure. I said to Liam Tuohy, "What are we going to do?" He says, "I'm going to hand out a few sets of rosary beads and let everyone say a few prayers."'

Brian Kerr, on the semi-final of the 1984 World Youth Cup against Russia.

'Liam made his point through humour, "Ray, my missus can run quicker than you", which was probably a fact.'

Ray Treacy, quoted in Sean Ryan, *The Boys in Green* (1997).

'Jack came into the dressing room during the home game against Iceland and started telling Liam's team how to play. For five years, Liam had been telling them to pass the ball, and now Jack was telling them to play the long ball. Liam resigned on the way home, and Noel O'Reilly and myself went with him. I had no dealings with Jack after that.'

Brian Kerr, on the row between Jack Charlton and Liam Tuohy.

'After Tuohy's resignation I was left with bloody inter-national sides all over the place. I didn't know anybody in Ireland. I didn't know anybody in the office. I didn't know anybody on the football side over here and I'm left with whole bloody thing. And Tuohy just dropped me on my head. Liam made a big bloody mistake. He could have been on the inside and now he's on the outside. Now, with everything that I have achieved the one thing that gives me great pleasure is that I stuffed it up his backside. That gives me great pleasure. Whatever I've achieved here is with no help from him. And I want people in this country to understand that.'

Jack Charlton.

'I hope I'm not such a sad b—d that I won't be able to have a life.'

Liam Tuohy, talking about his retirement.

Luck

Soccer supporters understand luck, but haven't a notion how to measure it. They define it by the statistical chances of having goals disallowed and refereeing decisions go against you. What does luck rhyme with?

'He epitomised this changing era because in truth he didn't really know what he was doing and – as a nation – neither did we. However whatever it was it was working. Big Jack forgot the names of players, made illegible notes about opponents on the back of cigarette packets and brooked no nonsense. He had the quality Napoleon most looked for in a general – and which Brian Kerr lacked – luck. Jack managed to qualify us for our first tournament by watching eleven Bulgarians commit suicide at home to a Scottish team who had all the dexterity of the Wombles. We couldn't believe our luck but were ready to commence the biggest party of our lives by repeatedly beating all comers nil-all.'

Dermot Bolger.

'That boy Abramovich will end up broke. He'll be selling programmes at Chelsea. He's only got 6 billion!'

Eamon Dunphy.

'My mother used to say I'm lucky but I'm not so sure. I always wanted to win.'

Billy Bingham.

'If you had to name one particular person to blame, it would have to be the players.'

Theo Foley.

'The dice were stacked against us.'

Theo Foley.

'It is not for me to make excuses, but they had all the luck and we had none.'

Terry Neill.

'I'm not a believer in luck but I do believe you need it.'

Fran Fields.

'Luck always played a part in Charlton's success, no matter how he disliked admitting it.'

Sean Ryan, *The Boys in Green* (1997).

'You never get everything you want out of football. I never want luck. I don't believe in luck. All I want is a fair crack of the whip.'

Jack Charlton.

Managers, Management and the Managed

Ireland has had ten managers, and they happen to be some of the most loquacious in the history of the game. They have no shortage of advice on how to do one of the most difficult jobs in European soccer.

'Ah yes, the boss.'
Pope John Paul II, to Jack Charlton during Papal audience at Italia '90.

'I am the boss, I am the gaffer. The buck stops with me.'
Steve Staunton on being appointed Ireland's manager (2006).

'Johnny Carey's situation as Irish manager was different from being a club manager. Quite often he'd turn up and find players missing, pulled out by their clubs on the pretext of an injury even though they could play the following Wednesday. He was very calm about it, but deep down he must have been seething.'

Charlie Hurley, quoted in Sean Ryan, *The Boys in Green* (1997).

'He did not always back the players. We could not even get a decent bus from the Gresham to Dalymount. That wouldn't bother him, but it bothered me.'

Noel Cantwell, on Johnny Carey, Ireland manager 1955-67, quoted in Sean Ryan, *The Boys in Green* (1997).

Journalist: 'You're making him sound very old.'

Kevin Kilbane: 'Well he is, inne?'

Discussion about Steve Staunton when he was captain at 2002 World Cup finals.

'Stan loves playing. He is always banging on the door saying, "Why wasn't I on the bench? Why wasn't I in the team? I can't believe you've left me out.'

John Gregory, former manager of Aston Villa.

'I love Stan. The only think that annoys me about him is that he gets up at half seven every morning for breakfast (he blames having kids) and never stops talking about the game.'

Jason McAteer.

'Stan, as we call him, must have been found beneath a rainbow.'

Vincent Hogan, journalist, writing during 2002 World Cup finals.

'Fractious, self-absorbed and overpaid, we woke to find ourselves as fourth seeds among countries we couldn't locate on maps. High-flying dreams are over and we have the downbeat, no-nonsense Steve Staunton to lead us from the wilderness as we wake up to the reality that the rest of the world doesn't necessarily love us anymore. We don't know what the future holds, just where it begins – the mean streets of Dundalk.'

Dermot Bolger, on the appointment of Steve Staunton.

'I want to be successful so I'll want to beat Bohemians, Shelbourne and Dublin City. I'd beat my granny up and down the garden if that's what it takes.'

Roddy Collins, at his unveiling as the new manager of Shamrock Rovers.

'Eoin Hand was a decent, honourable man, done out of initial success by a colluding sect of dodgy referees who were not only Free Masons but possibly Devil Worshippers too.'

Dermot Bolger.

'I've learned how to relieve managerial stress. When the ball gets into your last third, avert your eyes. Turn to your physio, ask for chewing gum, have a few words about the match, anything. It stops the tension building up. You might miss a goal but someone will always tell you how it happened.'

Billy Bingham (1992).

'I've heard it said that you can't be a football manager and tell the truth. Well, I'm going to have a go at it.'

Liam Brady.

'A manager is there to be seen and exposed to his players. They will know him within seven days. They will sort out his strengths and weaknesses immediately.'

Eamon Dunphy, *Only a Game* (1976).

'Mick McCarthy took them within sight of the World Cup quarter-final and he got the push. Brian Kerr got them within a point of qualifying and he got the push. I'm glad I'm not applying for the job.'

Jack Charlton (December 2005).

'There are only two certainties in this life. People die and managers get the sack.'

Eoin Hand (1980).

'I am not in the habit of putting myself in places where I am unwanted and I have no intention of going forward for another term as manager. The job is too demanding and my immediate plans are not relative to international football.'

Eoin Hand, announcing his resignation as Ireland manager after a 2-0 defeat in Moscow.

'Peter Doherty used to fire us up with tales of heroic Irish victories from years ago. The thing was, when we looked up the record books they were usually defeats.'

Danny Blanchflower.

'I left as I arrived, fired with enthusiasm.'

Roddy Collins (attrib.)

'It seems you can get sacked for farting in the wrong direction at the moment.'

Joe Kinnear, Wimbledon manager, after Kenny Dalglish's departure from Newcastle.

'I like being manager of Wimbledon. I don't think there's any challenge in being manager of AC Milan.'

Joe Kinnear.

'Peter Doherty brought a wind of change into the Northern Ireland dressing room. He showed us how quickly the outlook could alter once a team became united in its desire to improve things. Anybody can become better once they set their minds and energies to that end.'

Danny Blanchflower.

'It's like going into a nuclear war with bows and arrows.'

Joe Kinnear, on Wimbledon's lack of spending power (1995).

'You have to be a bit of everything these days: coach, social worker, the lot. If Claire Raynor knew soccer, she'd be a great manager.'

Mick McCarthy (1995).

'I told the chairman that if he ever wants to sack me, all he has to do is take me into town, buy me a meal, a few pints and a cigar, and I will piss off.'

Mick McCarthy, talking when he was manager of Millwall (1995).

Reporter: 'Who is your favourite manager?'

George Best: 'The manager at Stringfellows.'

'If we played like that every week we wouldn't be so inconsistent.'
Roddy Collins (May 2000).

'I like to breed players that attack people.'
Dave O'Leary.

'Welcome to the grey hair club.'
Kevin Keegan, sending a message to John Aldridge when he became Tranmere player-manager (1996).

'The best thing I could do now is head off and play golf.'
Pat Byrne, resigning as Kilkenny City manager after being banned by the FAI from any ground in which his team are playing (February 2000).

'I thought John McCarthy was having an absolute stinker. It was only when I was going to take him off that I was told that he had been sent off five minutes earlier.'
Roddy Collins.

I'd love to pull the strings of a big club, players, listen to people. I look at our manager [Alex Ferguson] and I think about it. I know it's stressful. People will say, if I'm going to walk away from this, what chance do I have of being a manager? I don't know. I think I'd enjoy that challenge. At the end of the day, I enjoy managing myself regarding looking after myself, stretching, weights. I'd enjoy stretching that. Good players and good people with me, people I could trust. I'd like that.'

Roy Keane, on management.

'Once you are national team manager you are public property. People go to matches, they own a part of you.'

John Giles, quoted in Paul Rowan, *The Team That Jack Built* (1994).

'Everything I do in club football will be just part of the apprenticeship until I get the Ireland job.'

Roddy Collins.

'Glenn Hoddle's career in management has been a bit of a mixed grill.'

John Giles.

'If there are any further questions I will be at my desk at ten in the morning.'

Andy Roxburgh, Scotland manager, after Ireland beat Scotland 1-0 (1987).

'Everything in our favour was against us.'

Danny Blanchflower.

'A good manager will make eleven players look like a good team. Whereas a bad manager will make eleven players look like a bad team.'

John Giles.

'Germany, like ourselves, have been in transition, but they still qualified for the World Cup.'

Steve Staunton, Irish team manager, before the 2006 World Cup finals, for which Germany qualified as hosts.

'I'm out at the moment, but should you be the chairman of Barcelona, AC Milan or Real Madrid, I'll get straight back to you. The rest can wait.'

Joe Kinnear's answer-phone message (1995).

Manyoo and the Manyoo-er Heap

In the absence of a strong soccer culture of their own, Irish people have acquired a penchant for supporting clubs from outside Ireland. Nobody has explained satisfactorily what makes Manchester United one of the four most supported cross-channel clubs in Ireland, perhaps the most supported, because it is difficult to enumerate exactly what defines a supporter of Manchester United, Liverpool or Celtic. The literature of Manchester United and the achievements of their players (and manager) from Ireland have given it a folklore of its own.

'I even judge people's characters on whether they support Manchester United.'

Ardal O'Hanlan, comedian.

'Matt Busby loved Dublin, sensing a part of his past in its carefree, infectious informality, and Dalymount was one of his favourite nights, his young side doing him proud with football that was elegant, precise and, for those of us who watched from the terraces, unbelievably grand.'

Eamon Dunphy, *A Strange Kind of Glory* (1991).

'They had done it they were proud and they had every reason to be. And then they sat back and you could almost hear the energy and ambition sighing out of the club. It was not the willingness to win that had disappeared completely. It was still there. But after the European Cup it didn't seem quite so important. It was like being in at the winding up of a company.'

George Best.

'When it comes to the Red Devils Ireland is united. Not only the club's supporters, but a tremendous amount of playing talent as well. Ireland has contributed to the United cause.'

Chris Moore, *United Irishmen* (1999).

'Some people come to Old Trafford and I don't think they can spell football, let alone understand it. They have a few drinks and a prawn sandwich and don't realise what's going on out on the pitch.'

Roy Keane (2000).

'The first Irish were brought to Manchester by the De Traffords. They were a Catholic family, and persecuted for it at the time of the Reformation, but they were the biggest landowners in the area and own the ground where United play, Old Trafford. The De Traffords brought the educated Irish as doctors, lawyers, solicitors and priests and they built a foundation in the community for the workers who came at the time of the industrial revolution.'

Harold Riley, quoted in Eamon Dunphy, *A Strange Kind of Glory* (1991).

'Frank O'Farrell's integrity was well known in the game. In the age of dodgy deals and Flash Harrys, O'Farrell played by the rules and eschewed big talk. He is a man of absolute honour, unworldly to a degree. Everything must be done the right way. The belief in integrity, the fetish for doing things right was regarded a kink in his make-up. Of course there were compensations. Frank wouldn't f–k you. The problem was he wouldn't f–k anyone for you either.'

Eamon Dunphy, *A Strange Kind of Glory* (1991).

'The club is a kind of a reversal of the city's fate. Through it the lost capital of the industrial revolution is reborn.'

Fintan O'Toole.

'There are parts of the world where Manchester United are the only English words that people know.'

Eamon Dunphy.

'I suppose it was instinct really. The difference between a good player and a great player is that great players can read the game. That's something you cannot teach a guy. He either had it or he hasn't. And if he has he's halfway there. But you can't teach him to think.'

Billy Behan, Manchester United's Irish scout.

'Manchester United is everyone's second love.'
Frank O'Farrell.

'They were, or seemed, unearthly, handsome creatures from another planet, more heroic than any movie star we'd seen or could imagine. The following Saturday they lost to Wolves in the league.'
Eamon Dunphy, *A Strange Kind of Glory* (1991).

'We were destined to win the European Cup.'
George Best.

'All I wanted to do afterwards was to get away to some pub where I could sit quietly in a corner and drink some beer.'
Tony Dunne, after Manchester United won the European Cup (1968).

'You get greedier every season and you want to win everything.'
Roy Keane.

'Manchester United has rubbed off on me. I feel its glamour already. I feel, too, as great need to help the club back to its famed and feared reputation.'
Frank O'Farrell.

'I never felt that I ever let the team down or that I let myself down on the field. A lot of things were happening off the field that maybe I would have changed. I left Manchester United with a clear conscience.'
George Best.

'Over the years a lot of great players have left United – I'm sure the same will happen to me one day.'
Roy Keane.

'I look upon Frank as my last great signing, possible the greatest of the lot.'
Matt Busby, on appointing Frank O'Farrell as manager of Manchester United (1971).

'Nice day for an execution.'
Frank O'Farrell, on the morning he was sacked by Manchester United (1972).

'He came like a stranger and went like a stranger.'
Denis Law, on Frank O'Farrell.

'Death by a thousand cuts.'
Frank O'Farrell.

'Frank O'Failure.'
Newspaper headline.

'We were not a tactical side. We just played. We should have won more than we did.'
Tony Dunne.

'I left Bobby Charlton out of the side. Fair enough, I expected some reaction with a player as popular as Bobby involved. But the letters I got. They came from all over the world. And all telling me I was wrong. That's when you realise how many people are looking at you when you get a reaction like that.'

Frank O'Farrell.

'The Red Devils were different to those who'd come before them. No baggy shorts, but neat white pants, hitched up the perfect muscles on thighs of unimaginable power. They wore v-necked red shirts without the old collars of Matthews and Finney, trim and dashing, an emblem of the gods whose lithe bodies they adorned. Football never came to life so vividly, with such awesome beauty as it did that night in '57.'

Eamon Dunphy, *A Strange Kind of Glory* (1991).

'The only thing I have in common with George Best is that we come from the same place, play for the same club and were discovered by the same man.'

Norman Whiteside.

'Norman's from north Belfast, not the east, he's not romantic and he's got short hair.'

Bob Bishop, Manchester United's Belfast scout.

'Like winning the pools only to find you have forgotten to post the coupon.'

Sammy McIlroy, after the 1978 English FA Cup final.

'I always find it frustrating when my goal is shown on TV because you only see me taking the ball around the keeper. Alex had cleared the ball. David flicked it on and I stuck it through the centre-half's legs. I was more chuffed with that than anything. The keeper made my mind up for me by coming out quite quickly. So I took the ball around him. I thought about walking it in. Or stopping it on the line and kneeling down to head it in, but finally thought better of it.'

George Best, on his goal in the European Cup final.

'Alex Ferguson did receive an offer from Barcelona. The only other offer which has genuinely tempted him in recent years was the possibility of succeeding Jack Charlton as manager of Ireland. The Irish job interested him because he thought it would be a good way to spend the end of his career. He goes to Ireland often but the timing was wrong.'

Paul Wilson, journalist (October 2001).

'It's one of the things I wished to God I had the opportunity of doing – being manager of Manchester United.'

Noel Cantwell.

'I want to manager a massive club. If the Manchester United job comes available I will apply for it.'

Joe Kinnear.

Mick McCarthy

Ireland's ninth soccer team manager was born in Yorkshire and never lost the accent, adding to the comic effect of his one-liners. His career is not yet over and the final verdict on his stewardship of the national team has not been reached. One suspects it will be kinder than many of his contemporaries would allow.

'I was feeling as sick as the proverbial donkey.'
Mick McCarthy.

'Mick McCarthy, must be the world's highest-paid lift attendant.'
David Lacey (December 2005).

'We just have to crush Chelsea next week now we're on a roll.'
Mick McCarthy (January 2006).

'I'm a remarkably lucky fella to be doing the job I'm doing at the place I'm doing it, and I keep reminding myself of that. I've got nothing to bemoan my luck for, let me tell you, nothing at all in my life.'

Mick McCarthy.

'It wasn't a monkey on my back, it was *Planet of the Apes*.'

Mick McCarthy, talking after Sunderland's 2–0 win at Middlesbrough in September 2005 brought their first Premiership victory since December 2002.

'Well, it's a do not take £100 before passing Go matter, isn't it?'

Mick McCarthy, talking on Sky Sports when asked to compare David Ginola and Roy Keane, the winners of the Player of the Year awards in 1999 and 2000.

'I'm loving working with Mick. I find Mick very South Yorkshire, very honest indeed. He's very… I wouldn't say black and white, I would say red and white. There doesn't seem to be a bit of pink in the middle. If it's Friday today, it's Friday. He's slow to get his round in, but I'm really enjoying working with him.'

Bob Murray, Sunderland chairman.

'Hope and mathematics.'

Mick McCarthy, talking about Sunderland (December 2005).

'Here I am talking bull.'

Mick McCarthy, facing another press conference with the Irish team.

'It infuriates me that Mick McCarthy still isn't getting the accolades he deserves. Quite simply, he is the best manager that any Republic of Ireland team has ever had.'
Mark Lawrenson, talking during the 2002 World Cup finals.

'You can't buy talent like that. And even if you could, it would cost you a lot of money.'
Mick McCarthy, on Robbie Keane.

'Then I came to Millwall, a club with a chip on both shoulders.'
Mick McCarthy.

'We were forced to play so many youngsters that you had to burp and wind them after each game.'
Mick McCarthy, on managing Millwall (1996).

'That was a cross. If he meant it as a shot I'll drop my trousers in Burton's window.'
Mick McCarthy, while manager of Millwall, talking about a freak goal by Swindon's Jan Fjortoft (1995).

'People seem to think that Jack Charlton and me are exactly the same. But I was a forthright, blunt, arrogant b–d long before I ever got involved with him.'
Mick McCarthy (1995).

'We're football people, not poets, but obviously I'm disappointed with the result.'
Mick McCarthy.

'This is the greatest day ever at Lansdowne Road. Jack Charlton had better resources. But with the material he had, Mick McCarthy reduced the Dutch to a rabble.'

Eamon Dunphy, on RTÉ after Ireland's victory over the Netherlands in the qualifiers for the 2002 World Cup finals (2001).

'We are a bit of a motley crew. We can scrap and we can fight. But we can play as well.'

Mick McCarthy, after Ireland's victory over the Netherlands in the qualifiers for the 2002 World Cup finals.

'The Japanese gods were smiling on Ireland at Lansdowne Road, all eight million of them.'

Mick McCarthy, after Ireland's victory over the Netherlands in the qualifiers for the 2002 World Cup finals.

'They'd better take away his bootlaces, his belt and his tie after that.'

Mark Lawrenson, talking about Mick McCarthy after Ireland failed to qualify for the 2004 European Championship.

'Every single one of the players has been slapped around the head but they still keep coming back for more.'

Mick McCarthy, after Sunderland beat West Brom in their second league win of the [2005–06] season.

'Unless the club suddenly inherits £500 million or a relative of mine dies and leaves me £1 billion, players will be leaving.'

Mick McCarthy (2003).

'Happiness is not a condition that rests lightly on the Irish psyche. Rediscovering our Irishness under Mick McCarthy we quickly divided into bitter factions quarrelling over Roy Keane, house prices and infrastructure, as we grew disillusioned with newfound wealth.'

Dermot Bolger.

'There was a constant competition between myself and Mick McCarthy as to who could shout the loudest.'

Packie Bonner.

'I asked the players who wanted to take the penalty and there was an awful smell coming from some of them.'

Mick McCarthy.

Oops

Airtime given to soccer is so vast and the collections of broadcasting bloopers are now so common that it is hard for commentators to come up with an unintentional which is original. Someday soon, none of them will say anything sensible, such is the desire to be 'caught out'.

'The only man who can do anything for Ireland is sitting back in Cork.'
Eamon Dunphy, during the 2002 World Cup finals. As Roy Keane was in Manchester, who could he have been referring to?

'Some of the players never dreamed they would play at Wembley. Yet here they are today fulfilling those dreams.'
Lawrie McMenemy.

'Every time a side scores it can no longer be 0–0.'
Tom Tyrrell, Today FM commentator.

Niall Quinn

'He's the only referee that, when he makes a decision, there's no arms thrown into the air and no gestating.'
Niall Quinn.

'It's better than the old days, only better.'
Niall Quinn, quoted in *The Star*.

'With eight or ten minutes to go, they were able to bring Nicky Butt back and give him fifteen to twenty minutes.'
Niall Quinn.

'He managed to make a good hash of it in the end.'
Niall Quinn.

'I think Arsenal will win the game, but I think Everton have a real good chance.'
Niall Quinn.

'Everybody has been trying to put dots over T's and crossing over I's.'
Niall Quinn.

Frank Stapleton

'You've got to remember Damien Duff is one of the most good players in the Premiership.'
Frank Stapleton.

'You're not sure if the ball is going to bounce up or down.'
Frank Stapleton.

'A bit of retaliation there, though not actually on the same player.'
Frank Stapleton.

'He didn't get booked for the yellow card.'
Frank Stapleton.

'1–1 is probably a fair reflection of the score at half-time.'
Frank Stapleton.

'They're playing a 4–4–1–1–1 formation.'
Frank Stapleton.

Mark Lawrenson

'Ireland will give 99 per cent, everything they've got.
Mark Lawrenson.

'Manchester United have a dirge of central defenders.'
Mark Lawrenson.

'It's only a small place, Deportivo.'
Mark Lawrenson.

'They'll be playing 4–4–1–2…'
Mark Lawrenson.

'It's sometimes easier to defend a one-goal lead than a two-goal lead.'

Mark Lawrenson.

'If England get a point, it will be a point gained as opposed to two points lost.'

Mark Lawrenson.

'It's slightly alarming the way Manchester United decapitated against Stuttgart.'

Mark Lawrenson.

'England are numerically outnumbered in the midfield.'

Mark Lawrenson.

'The longer the game went on, you got the feeling that neither side really wanted to lose.'

Mark Lawrenson.

'There won't be a dry house in the place.'

Mark Lawrenson.

'Gary Neville was palpable for the second goal.'

Mark Lawrenson.

'It's like the Sea of Galilee – the two defenders just parted.'

Mark Lawrenson.

'To be a great game, one of the teams has to score first.'

Mark Lawrenson.

'They're in pole position, that is third position, for the Champions League.'

Mark Lawrenson.

'Michael Owen isn't the tallest of lads, but his height more than makes up for that.'

Mark Lawrenson.

'If you're a goalkeeper, it doesn't matter what you save the ball with – if you keep it out, it's not a goal.'

Mark Lawrenson.

'He can be as good as he wants to be, that's how good he can be.'

Mark Lawrenson.

'Most players would give their right arm for his left foot.'

Mark Lawrenson, on Jason Wilcox (1996).

'The number of chances they had before the goal they missed…'

Mark Lawrenson.

'If Plan A fails, they could always revert to Plan A.'

Mark Lawrenson.

'The problems at Wimbledon seem to be that the club has suffered a loss of complacency.'

Joe Kinnear.

'From now on, it's the start of a new beginning.'
Don Givens.

'He's on the lips of every team in world football.'
Ray Houghton.

'It was a good match, which could have gone either way and
very nearly did.'
Jim Sherwin.

'I was here at Maine Road when City lost 4–0 to Wimbledon,
but they could have been 2–0 up after five minutes, and if
they had been, the final score might just have been different.'
Jim Beglin.

'I am the manager at Macclesfield and want to give the job
my total commitment. Obviously as an Irishman I want the
job as Northern Ireland manager.'
Sammy McIlroy.

'That Johnny Giles of Leeds is a great player. Beats me why
Alf Ramsey has never picked him for England.'
Willie Ormond, Scotland manager (1973).

'A goal is going to decide this in many ways.'
David O'Leary.

'It was an excellent cross by Gary [Neville], I was surprised
by the quality of it.'
Roy Keane.

'I can count on the fingers of one hand ten games when we've caused our own downfall.'
Joe Kinnear (1993).

'Last week's match was a real game of cat and dog.'
John Aldridge on TV3.

'The Belgians will play like their fellow Scandinavians, Denmark and Sweden.'
Andy Townsend.

'I've seen on television on Sunday morning most days of the week.'
Jack Charlton.

'I don't think he's a thousand per cent mentally.'
Eamon Dunphy.

'The 3–5–3 system isn't working for them.
Eamon Dunphy.

'I think one or two of our legs got a bit leg-weary.'
Mick McCarthy.

'He lacks that confidence which he possesses.'
Martin O'Neill.

'I find the growing intervention by the football authorities in strictly footballing matters a rather worrying trend.'
Kenny Cunningham.

'Both sets of defenders are doing well for Deportivo.'
Mick Martin.

'It's a no-win game for us. Although I suppose we can win by winning.'
Gary Doherty.

'We seem to be a side that if we don't score we get beat.'
Jason McAteer.

'In the last ten minutes I was breathing out of my backside.'
Clinton Morrison.

'Nobody took the responsibility of going to kill Yakin.'
Packie Bonner.

'If in winning we only draw we would be fine.'
Jack Charlton.

'Even if he had scored for Alaves, it would have made no difference to the scoreline.'
Gerry Armstrong.

'All of Blackburn's players got their foots in.'
Eamon Dunphy.

'Roy Keane didn't go through the book with a fine toothbrush.'
Tony Cascarino.

'He's a great little player... who scored it again?'
Jack Charlton.

'It was a definite penalty but Wright made a right swansong of it.'
Jack Charlton.

'The Arsenal defence is skating close to the wind.'
Jack Charlton.

'Lovely little simple intricate passes.'
Noel King.

'The Waterford player's shot was on target, which is an important aspect of a players shot.'
Damien Richardson.

'The players with the wind will have to control it a bit more.'
Jack Charlton.

'Neil Lennon wasn't sent off for scoring a goal, and that's what annoys me.'
Martin O'Neill.

'The first 90 minutes are the most important.'
Jack Charlton.

'The best thing for them to do is stay at 0–0 until they score the goal.'
Martin O'Neill.

'It was a game we should have won. We lost it because we thought we were going to win it. But then again, I thought that there was no way we were going to get a result there.'
Jack Charlton.

'We probably got on better with the likes of Holland, Belgium, Norway and Sweden, some of whom are not even European.'
Jack Charlton.

'We rode our luck, but that's what the goalposts are there for.'
Joe Kinnear.

'When you are 4–0 up you should never lose 7–1.'
Lawrie McMenemy.

'The last player to score a hat-trick in an FA Cup final was Stan Mortensen. He even had a final named after him – The Matthews Final.'
Lawrie McMenemy.

'He's put on weight and I've lost it, and vice versa.'
Ronnie Whelan.

'Now the world is my lobster.'
Keith O'Neill.

'You can't wait until you are a goal down at half-time before you throw the gun at them.'
John Aldridge.

'I expect Chelsea to make a world-record signing in the near distant future.'

Tony Cascarino.

'I was a young lad when I was growing up.'

David O'Leary.

'Inter have bought the finished article and there's no doubt he can keep improving.'

Mick McCarthy.

'I've spoken to five managers in the past eight days and 85 per cent of them have called me to chat about my players.'

Martin O'Neill.

'If we had taken our chances we would have won, at least.'

David O'Leary.

'If it's not a contract I want then I won't sign it. That's not a threat.'

Roy Keane.

'If there's one thing Gus Uhlenbeek's got, it's pace and determination.'

Ray Houghton.

'Gomes had scored four goals for Portugal against Andorra, including a hat-trick.'

Bill O'Herlihy.

'Beckham, Keane and Ronny Johnsen are all missing through fatel [sic] injuries.'
RTÉ Teletext.

'With news of Ireland's 1–1 victory over Holland...'
RTÉ newsreader.

'There's an unmentionable four-letter word in Northern Ireland's World Cup vocabulary at the moment – defeat.'
Daily Mirror.

'There's only one club in Europe that you can leave Manchester United for – Real Madrid or Barcelona.'
John Aldridge.

'That's down to one thing, fitness and organisation.'
Noel King.

'Physically imposing, Rosenborg play a fluid 4–4–3 formation that has been honed over a twenty-year period.
Irish Independent.

'Brian, I know you've got your backbone set in stone.'
Damien Richardson.

'Let's see what RTÉ Sport has in the way of sport this week.'
Darragh Moloney.

'You should never have married Maradona.'
Man in Mulligan's of Poolbeg Street, talking to Sean Penn.

'[Jamie Redknapp is] not eligible for games infecting Premiership issues.'
RTÉ Teletext.

'We want a draw or as close as we can get to one.'
Cobh Ramblers fan.

'The PA man announced the winning ticket in the club lotto before adding that tickets were still available.'
Weblog, on a UCD away match.

'Freddie Ljungberg desperately wants to suck in Cocu.'
Andy Townsend, on ITV.

Dick Advocaat's furious. He has just kicked the bucket, I think.'
Andy Townsend.

'Once he has got confidence in his veins he is a real threat.'
Andy Townsend.

'This one was an early afternoon kick-off for both sides.'
Bill O'Herlihy.

'Maldini has really regurgitated his career at left-back.'
Damien Richardson.

'For my money, Duff servicing people from the left with his balls in there is the best option.'
Andy Gray.

'The overwhelming view of the listeners is that they are split down the middle.'
Eamon Dunphy.

'They've given themselves a mountain, er Mount Everest, which is just around the corner from here.'
John Aldridge in Basle, Switzerland.

'If you don't want to know the score in the other games look away now [caption shows 1–0], actually it is one-all now.'
Bill O'Herlihy.

'Newcastle have struggled to score goal on their travels, especially away from home.'
Ray Houghton.

'I was trying to fix it, when it came crashing down on top of me. The corner of the post seemed a bit loose so I jumped up to try and mend it.'
Mick O'Brien, Athlone Town goalkeeper, explaining why he broke the crossbar twice during the 1974 FAI cup semi-final and was sent off for his trouble.

'When I touched it the post came away in my hand. It is my habit to swing from the crossbar to make sure the ball went over, and to keep the crowd happy by doing somersaults in the goalmouth.'
Mick O'Brien.

'There is a third reason. I think I might be over-fit.'
Mick O'Brien.

'Ajax have players from all over the world, from Africa, Egypt, Belgium.'

Noel King.

'If Ireland had scored more goals they would have won the match.'

Jimmy Magee.

Party Animals

Footballers with youth, money and time on their hands have always been among the great socialisers of our time. It is the interest of club-owners, gossip writers and ordinary eyeballers that is new. The stories of the exploits of Irish teams until the 1990s have a barstool folklore of their own. But then someone discovered there was an endearing quality about the public celebration of the Irish teams and their fans.

'The Irish football and beer team.'
Description of Irish team at 1972 tournament in Brazil.

'Okay, everybody off. But let's be clear about this. I am not buying the drinks.'
Jack Charlton, allowing a stopover in a pub during the training camp for Euro '88. Quoted in *Tony Cascarino, Full Time: The Secret Life of Tony Cascarino* (2000).

'The Carlsberg ad is getting a little closer.'

Jason McAteer, after Ireland qualified for the last sixteen of the 2002 World Cup finals.

'We pretended to the world that we weren't to be taken seriously.'

Niall Quinn, *The Autobiography* (2002).

'Jack Charlton has installed a tough regime and insisted we were all in our beds at 5 a.m.'

Gary Kelly, talking at Italia '90.

'Italy turn up in Armani suits looking like the dog's bollocks and we turn up in bright green blazers and dodgy brogues.'

Phil Babb (1995).

'I only went over to complain about the noise.'

Dessie Cahill, on the Irish team party at the 2002 World Cup finals. He played a tape of the team and friends joining in a tuneless 'Boys in Green', admitting this was proof that there was serious 'disharmony in the camp'.

'I can't really remember what it was that I particularly liked about him. I had five pints of Guinness in the afternoon and it was all a bit blurred!'

Steve Coppell, Reading manager, on his scouting trip to Cork.

'A singsong in the hotel bar. Players, staff, families and fans all bound together in a great, rollicking din of well-being. The FAI opening a tab at the bar for everyone. The songs and the laughter. The sense of brotherhood. It was Alan

Kelly who nudged me. "Could you imagine," Alan grinned. "Sven Goran Eriksson and the English boys having a night like this?" And I couldn't. Not that England don't have their own special moments. Of course, they do. But this was so quintessentially Irish, so simple and unaffected, it just felt like a kind of shorthand for what we are as people.'

Vincent Hogan, about the 2002 World Cup finals.

'We're drowning our sorrows.'

Peter Doherty, Northern Ireland manager, when asked by a journalist why the team was having a party after being beaten.

'I drink to keep myself sane in what is a narrow, shallow world. Very little in football is authentic. Hands up how many Premiership footballers travelled on public transport this year. How many of us had to queue for anything? We've quarantined ourselves from the world. The pub has been my escape.'

Niall Quinn, *The Autobiography* (2002).

'There is no doubt we could have sacked him, but I'm pleased we haven't.'

Kevin Keegan, when he was the manager of Manchester City, after Ireland defender Richard Dunne turned up for training in a 'dishevelled' state.

'When we played England off the park at Wembley in 1991, every Irish player attended a PFA dinner until 2 a.m., less than 72 hours before kick-off. We were in full view of everyone and we are still lauded by the media for our display at Wembley. Last month, five days before France, a few of the Ireland team went out for a meal and after it a few of the few had a night out. There was a frenzy of media criticiom designed to embarrass the manager.'

Niall Quinn.

'Ray Treacy got 56 caps for Ireland. Thirty were for his singing.'
Eamon Dunphy

'"The Green Army came, saw, drank and conquered. Rarely have a team's fans achieved such an overwhelming victory overseas. They drink, but they do not get violent that's their pride," declared the headline in Monday's *Tokyo Shimbun* newspaper.'

Tom Clifford, journalist at the 2002 World Cup finals.

'Jack gathered us all in a circle. "Who is the f–ker with the bird in the room?" he demanded. "Come on, own up." He seemed reasonably calm at first but grew visibly more irritable with every negative response. One by one he put the question to everyone in the room but me. I couldn't believe it… He completely lost his head. "What, we're training for the f–king World up and you take a bird back to the room." A group of journalists had moved into range and I thought for f–k's sake Jack, keep your voice down. We don't want them to get wind of it. But how do you tell Jack Charlton to shut it when he's frothing at the mouth with rage. He grumbled and continued to seethe until at last it was delivered. "Well I hope she was f–king worth it." And that was it. That's how it ended.'

Tony Cascarino, *Full Time: The Secret Life of Tony Cascarino* (2000).

Paul McGrath

Everything about Paul McGrath was unusual, the manner in which his career developed, his colour (Dublin born and bred, unlike team-mates from more multicultural back-grounds) and a shy reticence that endeared him to the public. As the height of his career he was not just the most talented, but the most loved member of the Irish team. Everyone had a good word to say about him. Well, almost everyone.

'Oooh aah himself.'

Michael Carwood, sportswriter.

'Paul is one of the all-time greats, someone to compare with Bobby Moore. He has always been a very intimidating player. I used to tell him, "Just look your opponents in the face, smile at them and frighten them to death."'

Jack Charlton.

'For us Paul is the fly in the ointment. If he was stable, steady, I wouldn't have such an urgent need of Phil Babb. But it's always in the back of my mind that Paul might have more problems with his knees, or that he might not bloody well turn up for the World Cup.'

Jack Charlton.

'I told him my problem was whether to include appearance or disappearance money.'

Ron Atkinson.

'Paul's every bit as good as Franco Baresi. He seems to have a magnetic head, everything comes to him.'

Andy Townsend (1994).

'It's the last time I'll be involved at Lansdowne Road… unless they pick me for the rugby.'

Paul McGrath, after his testimonial match in Dublin.

'If I wasn't playing I would be putting slates on roofs back in Ireland. Playing has got to be better than that.'

Paul McGrath (1993).

'The worst binges occurred when McGrath and Whiteside took to the bars as a double act. As swallowers they could have been backed with even money against W.C. Fields and Rab C. Nesbitt. The less active they were professionally, the more hectic they tended to be socially.'

Alex Ferguson, *Managing My Life* (1999).

'Everything that has happened to me is like a dream. Being involved with Ireland across the world. Hearing people chant my name.'

Paul McGrath, quoted in Colm Keane, *Ireland's Soccer Top Twenty (2004)*.

'You couldn't have written the script. Obviously there are certain things I would like to have erased from the script. But I look back now and think: that's something that happened to me, that was the way my path was to lead me.'

Paul McGrath, quoted in Colm Keane, *Ireland's Soccer Top Twenty (2004)*.

'I love my knees.'

Paul McGrath, quoted in *Hot Press* magazine.

'Sometimes he'd look at me as if he wanted to smash my head off something.'

Paul McGrath, talking about Jack Charlton quoted in Colm Keane, *Ireland's Soccer Top Twenty (2004)*.

'I found him unreachable. Time and again I would have him in my office, attempting to bring home to him the damage that alcohol was doing to his life. He would just nod in agreement.'

Alex Ferguson, *Managing My Life* (1999).

'We would rather have a drunk Paul with us than no Paul at all.'

Irish team message to Jack Charlton.

'My dodgy knees are keeping me out of this match. I just hope people believe me when I say that.'

Paul McGrath, after he went absent in Cork before a qualifier against Albania for the 1994 World Cup.

'He's probably off in a hotel room somewhere with some bird and a bottle of vodka.'

Jack Charlton, who didn't believe him.

'A dream tie is often a nightmare waiting to happen.'

Paul McGrath before Ireland v. Liechtenstein (1995).

'Paul McGrath limps on water.'

Banner at match in 1997.

'It makes me so angry. There are people in this country supposed to be looking after Paul, his so-called friends. Instead they seem happier leading him astray.'

Jack Charlton.

Philosophers

Since Albert Camus said that all he knew most surely about morality and the obligations of man, he owed to football, the search has been on for the profound in the utterance of footballers and their camp followers. Then came Eamon Dunphy.

'You need dictatorships and poverty to produce great footballers.'

Eamon Dunphy, during the 2004 European Championship.

'Never in the history of the FAI Cup have a team wearing hooped jerseys lost in a final ending in the year 5.'

Home Farm programme note (1985).

'A footballer can never plan his career.'

Liam Brady (1986).

'Machiavelli was an Italian. Wasn't he, John? Who did he play for?'

Eamon Dunphy, during the 2004 European Championship.

'All thirteen thousand of us stood on the terrace, for fifteen, twenty minutes after the last player had vanished, after Houghton had returned, forlornly waving a Tricolour in salute, after Jack had come back out to stand and stare in wonder at us. Coffin ships, the decks of cattle boats, the departure lounges of airports. We were not a chosen generation, the realisation of a dream any longer. We were just a hiccup, a brief stutter in the system. Thirteen thousand of us stood as one on that German terrace, before scattering back towards Ireland and out like a river bursting its banks across a vast continent.'

Dermot Bolger, *In High Germany*, a play set during the 1988 European Championship finals (1990).

'Anyone who uses the word quintessentially during a half-time talk is talking crap.'

Mick McCarthy, after Niall Quinn made a suggestion during an international match (1998).

'I got twenty-three caps which was great really. But what was great about it was the people and the trips. The fun we had in Paris and Prague or whatever and the little jokes we played. When you are not involved, those are the things you miss. Because most of the time the actual playing tears your guts out. It worries you, frets you. Even the honour of it, which is something very proud, never really hits you at the time. To stand there, when you play for your country, hearing

the national anthem, with your parents and friends and relations in the stand, is the greatest thing in your life. But it is greater for them, because they are watching and enjoying it. At the time you never really feel it is happening to you. You enjoy the day before and the day after more.'
Eamon Dunphy, *Only a Game* (1976).

'The more I earned, the louder my conscience became.'
Niall Quinn (2002).

Dessie Curley: 'I haven't cried since I was a kid.'

Sharon Curley: 'You cried during the World Cup.'

Dessie Curley: 'Sober, Sharon! Sober!'
Roddy Doyle, *The Snapper* (1990).

'Winston Churchill, Lawrence Of Arabia, Elton John! Yiz can all go f–k yerselves.'
Character in pub after Ireland scraped a 1-1 draw with England during Italia '90, from Roddy Doyle, *The Van* (1991).

'The roof stayed on but the foundations were definitely damaged. We jumped, dived, skidded, waltzed. I hugged people I hadn't seen in years. I hugged people I hated. I hugged the table. When I got my breath back I realised that I was drunk.'
Roddy Doyle, giving his own description of watching the England match during the 1990 World Cup finals, from *My Favourite Year: A Collection of New Football Writing* edited by Nick Hornby (1993).

'June came. School closed. The opening match, Cameroon beat Argentina. The next day Arnotts on Henry Street sold all their Cameroon jerseys and the dry cleaners on Kilbarrack Road started a World Cup special offer – all your curtains cleaned for 35 pounds. It was looking good.'

Roddy Doyle, during Italia '90.

'Italy had more misses than Henry VIII.'

Bill O'Herlihy.

'Southampton is a very well run outfit from Monday to Friday. It's Saturday we've got a problem with.'

Lawrie McMenemy (1995).

'The cat's among the pigeons and meanwhile we're stuck in limbo.'

Bernie Slavin (1991).

'When Roy Keane was sent home from Japan with a flea in his shorts, it was assumed that his replacement, if any, would also be male, able-bodied, aged roughly between 18 and 35, and capable of playing football. This, as will be obvious to all but the most politically dissolute readers of this newspaper, is a deeply sexist, healthist, ageist, professionalist and sportist notion.'

John Waters, journalist, during the 2002 World Cup finals.

'The cup final is a great occasion until ten minutes before the kick off. Then the players come on and spoil the whole thing.'

Danny Blanchflower.

'Though winning matters desperately, and we ache when we lose, they give life to the cliché that taking part is what matters and all of that seeps through into the way we understand everything else about the way we live.'

Gene Kerrigan, journalist, during the 2002 World Cup finals.

'My advice for young players? Drink lots of beer and smoke lots of fags.'

Gerry Taggart (2001).

'He doesn't piss in the sink like the rest of us.'

Shay Brennan, on Steve Heighway, who had a degree in Russian studies when he joined the Irish team.

'Germany are a very difficult team to beat. They had eleven internationals out there today.'

Steve Lomas, Northern Ireland captain (1999).

'At the end of the day it is all about what we do on the night.'

Bryan Hamilton, Northern Ireland manager, before a game against Germany (1996).

'Can the innocence of a nation delighted with what other countries would regard as failure be recaptured?'

Fintan O'Toole (2001).

'The sad truth is, for some men at least, that in the match between sex and football, football will always scrape through on goal difference.'

Joseph O'Connor, The Last of the Irish Males (2001).

'Without children, without dreams, without fans, football is just another way of spending time, wasting time. Its real force in society, its value to the culture is the richness of the relationship between the people's imaginings and dreams and the game itself.'

Eamon Dunphy.

'The flags are waving and no doubt at the foot of the Alps the cowbells are chiming too. And it is going to take a lot for Ireland to sour the chocolate.'

George Hamilton, during Ireland's Euro 2004 game in Basle.

'Kevin Moran, oldest man on the pitch today, thirty-five years of age, of course the referee could possibly be older than that, and technically he is on the pitch too, but then again his linesman could be even older than him, but are they technically *on* the pitch?'

George Hamilton.

'If the remnants of my classical education at the not so gentle hands of the Christian Brothers of Donore Avenue and Drimnagh Castle serve me correctly, it was that Greek playmaker of old, Epicurus, who stated that the misfortune of the wise is better than the prosperity of the fool.'

Damien Richardson.

'The last miles home on a long journey appear unending at the best of times, but traffic congestion when in sight of the homeland only serves to test further the resolve of those concerned.'

Damien Richardson.

Ray Stubbs: 'Will Greece lightning strike twice in the final?'

Mark Lawrenson: 'Not unless the referee is going to be a homer.'

'It seems that Portugal have replaced the artists with the artisans.'
Martin O'Neill.

'The team that Keane should have led went on to make his point for him. They provided us with a superb image of the collective strength within which individual brilliance could blossom. They gave the lie to the notion that personal luminosity and communal values are necessarily at odds.'
Fintan O'Toole, journalist, during the 2002 World Cup finals.

'Whether one possesses the stoical stature of an empirical philosopher or a more mundane propensity for self-gratification, the cataclysmic effect of one's removal from pole position in the most senior league in the country could be most injurious.'
Damien Richardson.

'History is today and tomorrow.'
Eamon Dunphy, asked about the legacy of Roy Keane.

Pioneers

The Scottish game, as soccer was known, came to Ireland just as two other handling codes were gaining in popularity. It got a foothold in the cities and urban areas where soldiers were to be found, and there it remained for most of its existence. A map of soccer Ireland in 1900 would have held true in 1980. There are those who ascribe the lack of success of Irish soccer teams to the largely disenfranchised constituency it served. As soccer moved from the fringes of Irish society into the focus of popular culture from 1988 on, this was expected to change. What would the first footballers have made of it all?

'Alexander cricket club v. the association section of Ulster cricket club.'

Notice, announcing the first match on the island in 1876 in Limavady, three years earlier than was claimed by McAlery.

'Yesterday these two well-known Glasgow clubs Queen's Park and Caledonians played an exhibition in the Ulster cricket ground, Belfast, under Scottish association rules with a view to the introduction of the association game into Ireland.'
Northern Whig (25 October 1878).

'All this has come upon us because of the hidebound prejudice of five men who select the teams preventing anyone outside the close circle of Belfast being chosen to represent his country. Northern prejudice is the bane of Irish football.'
Leinster delegate, after Ireland lost to England 13–2 (1898).

'Free State football is not recognised as first class.'
Football Sports Weekly (1924).

'It was very difficult for me to believe that I was as good as the English players and that is why I never did myself justice in England.'
Charlie Dowdall, of Leeds.

'Pat O'Callaghan put the Tricolour flying here for the 1928 Olympics. It is up to you lads to see it's still flying high this evening.'
Val Harris, trainer of 1932 Irish team.

'A handful of spectators and a stray dog.'
Description of attendance at first Leinster Cup final between Shelbourne and Tritonville, during one of several splits in Irish soccer history (1912).

'At the moment when a letter had been read from the English FA threatening to disturb international friendly relations if our claims were conceded, the representatives of Italy and Switzerland, placing right before might and justice in front of expediency, paced the way for recognition of our claims.'

Robert Murphy, FAI president, writing in *Football Sports Weekly* (1924).

Poets, Playwrights
and Writers

It took soccer a long time to impact on Irish writing. Although Joyce and Behan acknowledged its importance, it was the new generation of 1980s writers who began to focus on what was happening in Irish life. The writings varied between soccer's impact on gritty urban characters already traumatised by change and nostalgic recollections of simpler times when junior soccer served as an alternative to the mundanity of scratching out an existence.

'We have seen enough of the desert, it is time to book our place at the oasis.'

Irish Independent editorial.

'It was Kipling who spoke of "waiting and not being tired of waiting".'

Vincent Hoey, Drogheda United chairman, after his side's historic FAI Cup triumph.

'Success comes secondary, success to me without applying the ideals of the beautiful game that is soccer is a little bit hollow. League of Ireland football has for far too long held itself back, it's chained itself in its desire for success when in reality the success is an incestuous success. It is a home-based success that doesn't really impress people.'

Damien Richardson.

'Henceforth let it be known as 'Gloomsday', because there can be no doubt that Spain's undeserved World Cup victory over Ireland took the sheen off Bloomsday 2002. And that Spanish win had the unpleasant tang of fried kidney about it.'

Patsy McGarry, on Ireland's exit from the 2002 World Cup finals, *The Irish Times*.

'Seven Irish penalties in Suwon, then, perhaps the ugliest stadium of the World Cup. Four missed. Just tugs on a fruit machine to shape the nation's destiny.'

Vincent Hogan, *Irish Independent*.

'We spent a lot of time running into the bushes getting the ball back.'

Paul Mercier, on the filming of *Studs* (2006).

'The crowd joined in, every one of them, from Dublin and Cork, from London and Stockholm. And suddenly I knew this was the only country I still owned, those eleven players in green shirts, the menagerie of accents pleading with God.'

Dermot Bolger, *The Tramway End* (1993).

'The rumble of the studs on stage alone sent shivers up critics' spines.'

Fiachra O'Gibbons, critic, on the reaction to Paul Mercier's 1986 stage play *Studs*.

'We just got beaten. But it was the quality of the loss, that's what I always said – and we'd some great losses.'

Brendan Gleeson, actor, on the film version of *Studs* (2006).

'It begins in pre-history. Dinosaurs of Green open-decked buses prowl the length of O'Connell Street. A cluster of young men meet, some for the first time, outside the Gresham Hotel. They board a mini-bus which is just moving off when another unfamiliar figure with footballing boots runs down the darkening street. "Wait for me," he shouts, "I've been selected too."'

Dermot Bolger.

'Now the guys are all working – but one of them is getting a barracking off his supervisor in the supermarket, another guy's dad is getting on his case all the time, another is working so hard he's just trying to get away from the job. So, in a way, the situation hasn't changed, the football is still as pivotal for these fellas, even if there was far more despair in the 1980s.'

Paul Mercier, on the film version of *Studs* (2006).

'The line-up of the Republic of Ireland on 18–6–1994. Packie Bonner. Denis Irwin. Phil Babb. Paul McGrath. Terry Phelan. Ray Houghton. Andy Townsend. Roy Keane. John Sheridan. Steve Staunton. Tommy Coyne.'

Mary Hannigan, in a poem about that World Cup win over Italy (6 December 2004). She was inspired by the German poet Peter Handke who penned 'The Line-up of FC Nuremberg on 27-1-1968', an ode that contains no more than the names of the eleven Nuremberg players who lined up that day.

'No footballers were harmed during the making of the film.'

Closing credits on the film version of Studs (2006).

'We have missed those summers of 1988–94 not just for what was happening in Germany or Italy or the US, but for what was happening here. We remember, through the glowing mist of nostalgia, a time when words that have always been very complicated – society, community, identity – were, for a time, marvellously simple. When class barriers seemed to fall before the camaraderie. When waving the Tricolour was a token neither of defiance nor aggression but of easy allegiance. When strangers talked to each other because there was something in common to talk about. When the petty irritations and chronic anxieties of life were dissolved into one big, harmless anxiety.'

Fintan O'Toole (2001).

Politicians

Soccer has spawned more political rhetoric, and indeed more politicians, than it cares to admit. The Chichester family in Northern Ireland were among its first patrons. Seán Lemass, Todd Andrews, Osmonde Esmonde and Oscar Traynor were among the founders of the new state and Brian Lenihan and Bertie Ahern both played at a reasonable level. The President of Ireland first attended a soccer match in 1938, and the tradition has been maintained since. When Ireland beat the Soviet Union in 1974, the team was brought in their tracksuits to meet the president for the first time. A decade later, it had become popular for politicians to identify with winning soccer teams and stage-managed homcomings from major championships.

'You are children of the diaspora.'
Mary Robinson, talking to the Irish team on their return from the 1994 World Cup finals.

'Jason McAteer looked puzzled. Di Asporra, never heard of him. Must be an Italian defender who didn't make the squad, he seemed to think.'

Irish Press.

'I know he's a real football fan. He played for Drums and he knows his sport.'

Eamon Dunphy, on Taoiseach Bertie Ahern.

'Anywhere there is a ball kicked, a hurley swung or an opinion sought, you can count on Bertie to be there. He is the quintessential A.N. Other. The man who can fill the breach, do the business, make his points and, now and again score the odd own goal.'

Miriam Lord, on Bertie Ahern's appearance on RTÉ, *The Premiership* (September 2001).

'Considering that the economy is grinding to a halt, the health services are in chaos, the teachers are revolting, all our cities are gridlocked and while all this is happening our leader seems more worried about the deficiencies of the United back-four perhaps we should make an exception, encourage him to give up the day job and take up soccer punditry full-time.'

Kevin O'Shaughnessy, *Irish Independent.*

'You know, you can only lose between four and six matches if you're going to win the Premiership, erm, and that's two down after three matches.'

Bertie Ahern, television soccer analyst, on RTÉ, *The Premiership* (September 2001).

'Taoiseach, is this a sending off offence?'

Eamon Dunphy.

'Wes Brown's a great player, Silvestre's a great player, the two Nevilles are good enough for either side [interruption from Dunphy: "Silvestre's a good player, not a great player."] it should be good, but look at the amount of goals they've been giving away. They've given away a lot of goals. In most matches they've given away two goals.'

Bertie Ahern, television soccer analyst, on RTÉ, *The Premiership* (September 2001).

'All you had to do was hear him say that Manchester United's Mikael Silvestre was a great player to realise that now and again he can be guilty of slack marking in his opinions.'

Miriam Lord, on Bertie Ahern's appearance on *The Premiership* (September 2001).

'I think, erm, he, he certainly gave two swings, erm, and the second one is certainly the upper-cut... erm, watch the swing back on the second one... a straight elbow into the face.'

Bertie Ahern, television soccer analyst, on RTÉ, *The Premiership* (September 2001).

'Up popped Shay Given on the screen followed by Jason McAteer and finally, wait for it, Bertie Ahern! Drapier couldn't believe his eyes. The message was clear: Bertie 2 Iran 0. Is there nowhere safe from this man?'

Drapier, *The Irish Times* (November 2001).

'If you have bad news you want to bury, today's the day to have a press conference and announce it. About two o'clock this afternoon would be perfect. If the government wants to privatise the fire brigade or put taxi meters on ambulances, watch out today is the day.'

Gene Kerrigan, on the day of Ireland v. Spain in the 2002 World Cup finals.

'Bertie Ahern got the gift he always wanted at the match – a Russian away strip. It's not as nice as the Man U strip, but it'll do for jogging when the other one is in the wash.'

Miriam Lord (2002).

'We never qualified for the World Cup. In our day, you didn't see the Taoiseach at our matches.'

Johnny Giles.

'Maybe Niall Quinn will be there one day, as president, shaking hands.'

Johnny Giles, commenting on the homecoming ceremony after the 2002 World Cup finals.

'Gaelic football is a game that I have very little esteem or regard for. I would prefer to look at other games, but I know that, with the exception of the cities of Cork, Limerick and Dublin, it is the game universally played in the Twenty-Six Counties.'

Seán McEntee, Dáil Éireann (July 1931).

'Everybody who knows anything about Association football knows, that the directors of these big Association football

clubs actually engage in buying and selling Irishmen and in
deporting Irishmen across Channel to the great Association
football clubs over there.'
William Davin, Dáil Éireann (July 1931).

'We all know that Association and Rugby football are
generally played on a Saturday, and that their supporters are
the moneyed classes.'
Dan Corry, Dáil Éireann (July 1931).

'The Soccer Association, which previously was looked upon
as somewhat of an English and shoneen association, because
of the fact that it was an English game in those days, and was
played by the British Army, is now largely played by the very
poor working classes of the towns. People would hardly
accuse the people of Ringsend and that section of Dublin,
who are amongst the most enthusiastic supporters of the
Rovers and the Shelbournes, of being snobbish.'
Osmonde Esmonde, TD and FAI president, Dáil Éireann
(June 1931).

'There is no conflict between the GAA and the Soccer
Association, because the GAA is there for a very definite
purpose – to develop Irish national games. The Soccer
Association is there to uphold, in the international language
of football, the honour of our country.'
Osmonde Esmonde, TD and FAI president, Dáil Éireann (July
1931).

'At any time in Dalymount Park or any of the principal parks
in this city you will see 30,000 people at these matches –

members of the National Army, members of the Old IRA and followers of certain forms of sport who are not supposed to be there, according to their rules, but are there all the same. The Irish Government should face up to their responsibility. I can assure them that it was a sight worth seeing when 30,000 – on one occasion 32,000 – were at a football match, and when the National Anthem of this country was played they stood with their hats off and most of them joined in it themselves. We have Ministers of State who enjoy these soccer matches. The Government should, once and for all, in case there is any prejudice against it, face the fact that the country as a whole desires no prejudices so far as the sport of the country is concerned.'

John Joseph Byrne, Dáil Éireann (June 1941).

'If Linfield football team are beaten by Shamrock Rovers, the ordinary people are taught that the Fianna Fáil Government are delighted. The fact that members of Fianna Fáil – as well as members of the Labour Party and Fine Gael – may never have heard of the Linfield football team does not impress them.'

Noel Browne, Dáil Éireann (October 1971).

'In the last two and a half weeks we have celebrated the success of the Irish soccer team in Italy. You may ask, Sir, what relevance has the Irish soccer team in Italy to this Bill. The overwhelming majority of people who have not been able to go to Italy have been sitting in front of their television screens watching what can only be described as the superb broadcast and television presentation by RTÉ Network 2 on a daily basis, with Bill O'Herlihy and the other members of the panel, Johnny Giles and Eamon Dunphy, whom some people like and some hate but who certainly adds a great deal of interest to the programmes.'

Alan Shatter.

'We are not at war with Argentina and we shouldn't be governed by the managers of British soccer teams as to who, how and when we play.'

Niall Andrews, during preparations for 1982 tour of South America, when many English clubs refused to release their players because of the Falklands War.

'Dunphy didn't have to go on the trip but he nearly knocked a nun over in the rush to the plane.'

Ray Treacy, on Eamon Dunphy's campaign to boycott the 1974 away match with Chile, quoted in Paul Rowan, *The Team That Jack Built* (1994).

Pundits

It seems hard to imagine now, but finding articulate ex-players prepared to come on and speak coherently about matches was long a problem for masters of the small screen. Then came live television, lots of it, and Irish players and ex-players seemed to fill every studio. The viewer could now sit back and enjoy the discussion as much as the match, as the screen army tried a few variations on a winning formula: punter to ask the questions, serious analyst to answer them, and a clown for entertainment. With RTÉ's most famous team of Bill O'Herlihy, John Giles and Eamon Dunphy the three roles became interchangeable, and an inspiration for impresarios.

'I wouldn't like to see them depressed, if that was what they were like when they were celebrating.'

Pat Delaney, of the Small Firms Association, talking about RTÉ's television pundits.

'George from Sligo has just rung in to say that most countries in Euro 2000 play in a colour that appears in their national flag, why is it that Italy play in blue? Well George, I have to inform you that, as far as I know, the colours of the Italian flag are red, white and blue.'

Eamon Dunphy, Today FM (2000).

'Ireland has played three games without Roy Keane and RTÉ has played one without Eamon Dunphy and, to be honest, neither of them has been missed.'

John Boland, TV columnist, during the 2002 World Cup finals, *Irish Independent*.

'Oi, Montrose, ye've got yer apology, now reinstate him, yer midfield lacks a leader.'

Mary Hannigan, TV analyst, *The Irish Times*.

'I was expecting Hans Christian Andersen to come on.'

Gerry Armstrong, analysing a Danish victory.

'You can only call the match as you see it on previous evidence.'

John Giles.

'Watching him presenting TV3's Champions League coverage, the conflict seems to rage within his very being, with his mind trying to concentrate on the football, while his eyes dart all over the place. We sense that he is seeing things he does not understand, things which we can't see, but which, if they were visible to us, would fill us with terror.'

Declan Lynch, on Packie Bonner's presentation on TV3.

'What a proactive World Cup RTÉ are having. First they hire a contentious commentator whose bias against Mick McCarthy would seem to disqualify him for the job. Then they fire him for something as trivial as having a hangover. And then (and this is the weird bit) they immediately send a reporter and camera crew around to his house to find out how he feels about being fired by them. Only in Ireland. Only in Montrose.'

John Boland, TV reviewer, commenting on Eamon Dunphy's unhappy World Cup finals, *Irish Independent* (2002).

'If Saddam Hussein went on *The Late Late Show* he'd get a standing ovation.'

Eamon Dunphy, on the reception afforded Brian Kerr on RTÉ television.

'If you win this you won't have to do two years in the army.'

Mick McCarthy, speculating on the BBC how the South Korean manager motivates his team.

'If I was the manager of Denmark and the Swedish coach came to me and said, "We'll do it", if you were really ruthless, you'd say, "All right, we'll go first, we'll go one up, then 1–1" and then when we went 2–1 up we'd stuff 'em.'

Eamon Dunphy.

'We cannot fail to detect a fair amount of inverted provincialism in certain reports of sports. The most recent example I saw was in a soccer cup match in Cork between Shamrock Rovers and Cork Hibernians, where Cork Hibernians were the underdogs and surprised everybody by drawing the match one all. The goal shown on Telefís Éireann was not the one scored by Cork Hibs: it was the one by Shamrock Rovers. In general we have a feeling that this is quite characteristic.'

Professor Quinlan, Seanad Éireann (1966).

John Toshack: 'We could be in for the Greece–Latvia final. Ha ha.'

Stephen Cullinane: 'Yes. You never know. Stranger things have happened.'

John Toshack: 'No! No they haven't.'

Exchange on TV3.

Gary Lineker: 'Do you think Rio Ferdinand is a natural defender.'

Dave O'Leary: 'He could grow into one.'

Exchange during BBC TV's coverage of the 2002 World Cup finals.

Bill O'Herlihy: 'We've a big game tomorrow night. And of course it's a big game for us as well.'

John Giles: 'Yeah, let's hope everyone is watching.'

Bill O'Herlihy: 'You're very sarcastic tonight, John.'

John Giles: 'I'm not being sarcastic Bill. It's very important… ratings.'

Bill O'Herlihy: 'That's right, John.'

'Biggest mistake of the tournament from either channel: ITV allowing Mick McCarthy to co-commentate on the Sweden–

Denmark game, not realising that his voice is the most painful, gut-wrenching and hideous sound ever to grace this earth.'

From *Football 365*'s review of Euro 2004.

Bill O'Herlihy: 'No dissertations from you about tattoos or whatever tonight, Eamon?'

Eamon Dunphy: 'No, Bill, but I know where Beckham's tattoo came from.'

Bill O'Herlihy: 'No libel on air, Eamon, please.'

Eamon Dunphy: 'I'll tell you later then.'

Damien Richardson: 'Glenn Crowe, John O'Flynn, Stephen Geoghegan are great strikers – none of these players is trepidacious in front of goal.'

Trevor Welch: 'I like that word, Damien [turns to camera] – intrepidacious.'

Exchange on TV3.

'Football is the only sport I can watch with true pleasure. The game itself is a thing of blissful majesty, only slightly diminished by the ubiquitous pundits and commentators.'

Joseph O'Connor, *The Last of the Irish Males* (2001).

'It's 1–1, and if there are no more goals it will be a draw.'

Tommy Smyth.

'He's on the lips of every team in world football.'

Ray Houghton, on Damien Duff.

'It must be hard to convince yourself you're playing on the road when you're playing at home.'
Tommy Smyth.

'If either side was to draw tonight they'd still be favourites to go through.'
Frank Stapleton.

'Kilbane's head is better than his feet. If only he three heads, one at the end of each leg.'
Eamon Dunphy.

'Ireland should be allowed to draft in a replacement for Keane because he must have an injury of the brain.'
Ray Houghton.

'A mythical creature, half man and half moustache.'
Martin Kelner, journalist, on Des Lynam (2004).

'I'm sure Heinz will be in Karel Bruckner's thinking mind now.'
Andy Townsend.

'I felt there was a lack of definable objectivity about both teams.'
Damien Richardson.

'The Russians will be big and strong if you let them be big and strong.'
Damien Richardson.

'They said it was the group of death. In the end it was very much the group of survival. Especially for those who survived.'

Jimmy Magee.

'He's like a laxative. He just goes straight through you and there is nothing you can do about it.'

Andy Townsend.

'Last year you could have set your watch by the Liverpool back four, right back, two centre halves, left back.'

Ray Houghton.

'United go home having given one of the top Division Two sides a much more difficult day than most plaudits expected.'

Roddy Collins.

'Kilbane's like a one-eyed cat in a fish shop. He doesn't know what to do or where to go.'

Mark Lawrenson.

'He deserved the free kick but was fortunate to get it.'

Tommy Smyth.

Bill O'Herlihy: 'Carsley lacks a bit of skill in those situations. Let's call a spade a spade.'

John Giles: "Yes, Bill, he's in there to dig.'

'Juventus are waiting to remodelise their stadium.'

Trevor Welch.

'He can sometimes be the icing on the cake, but other times he is the piece underneath that nobody sees.'
Mark Lawrenson.

'Australia have failed narrowly to miss out on all the major competitions.'
Trevor Welch.

Bill O'Herlihy: 'This is a local derby between Germany and Holland.'

John Giles: 'Yeah, they've been close to each other for years.'

'West Ham have to weather the storm, although it was really only a tempest.'
Frank Stapleton.

Bill O'Herlihy: 'Sixteen days from now we'll all walk tall John.'

John Giles: 'I don't think we'll be any taller Bill.'

'These managers all know their onions and cut their cloth accordingly.'
Mark Lawrenson.

'I'm contemplating Totti in a sense.'
Bill O'Herlihy.

'The away team always want to get an away goal and at the same time the whole team like to keep a clean sheet. Know what I mean?'
Kevin Moran.

Bill O'Herlihy: 'What are you actually saying, John?'

John Giles: 'What am I saying?'

Bill O'Herlihy: 'Yeah.'

John Giles: 'I would be more confident that we could win this game now than before the game.'

Bill O'Herlihy: 'You could be a cock-eyed optimist.'

John Giles: 'I'm not.'

'He's not fast, but he's quick.'
Tommy Smyth.

Referees

Another problem with referees – finding something original to call them.

'I'm not going to have a go at the referee but he was a complete twerp.'

Jack Charlton.

'I criticise referees but I wouldn't want their job for a gold pig.'

Mick McCarthy (1995).

'As a footnote to the World Cup, it seems in retrospect that Ireland was fortunate in one respect in having no part of the proceedings. One of the linesmen for the final was a member of the West Midlands Police.'

Declan Lynch, talking about the 1998 World Cup finals.

'I believe when the referees are enjoying their recreation on the sunbeds or swimming up and down a pool and talking together in their free time, there is an agenda with Alan Smith. They all have their little chats and jump on him very, very quickly.'

David O'Leary, when he was Leeds manager (2002).

'Mick McCarthy shakes his head in agreement with the referee.'

Martin Tyler.

'I know where he should have put his flag up, and he'd have got plenty of help.'

Roddy Collins.

'The story of the representatives of Shelbourne and Bohemians at the League meeting was not exactly flattering to the gentlemen of the whistle in Dublin. We were told there was not a referee in Dublin capable of conducting a stiff game.'

Jack McAlinden, *Sport* (25 October 1920).

'There's no rapport with referees these days. If you say anything you get booked, and if you don't they send you off for dumb insolence.'

Jack Charlton (1983).

'Why should I allow a referee to do things which destroy my life? When managers make mistakes they get sacked. What happens a referee? He is probably going home in his car now thinking about where he is going to referee next week.'

Joe Kinnear.

'Keep it up and you'll need a new pea at half-time.'

Fan at Ireland v. Switzerland (1975).

Religious Affairs

For a sport codified at a time when people believed fervently in an interventionist God, it is no surprise that religious matters have occasionally impacted on soccer in Ireland and led to the comic scenario of one bishop attempting to get an international match called off.

'Religion has a lot to answer for. Looking back, I couldn't have told you whether most of my team-mates were Catholic or Protestant. We didn't give a damn about that sort of thing. '

Jimmy Jones, victim of a savage attack that put Belfast Celtic out of soccer.

'Damien Duff should take the Padre Pio medal out of his football boot in case he ends up with the stigmata on his foot.'

Caller to Today FM's *Sunday Supplement* during the 2002 World Cup finals.

'The archbishop, has heard with regret of the proposed match between Ireland and Yugoslavia and the proposed banquet. His Grace is sorry that the FAI had not the courtesy to approach him for his views and he hopes even at this late stage that the match might be cancelled.'

Message from Fr O'Regan, chancellor to John Charles McQuaid at the Archbishop's House in Dublin, in advance of a match between Ireland and Yugoslavia (1955).

'This matter is a sporting affair between two countries, and I am sure that the counterpart of the FAI in Yugoslavia have as much to say in the politics of that country as the association have here.'

Samuel Robert Prole, FAI president, responding to Archbishop McQuaid's request (1955).

'It is most regrettable that your association which so many tens of thousands of Irish Catholics are found has failed to realise how distasteful to Irish Catholics is this link with a communist dominated country.'

Letter from a Knight of Columbanus, opposing the match against Yugoslavia (1955).

'The arguments of those who plead that sport should be above politics is unrealistic in view of the uses to which sport is put in communist countries.'

Letter to FAI from the Guilds of Regnum Christi, opposing the match against Yugoslavia (1955).

'The Holy City.'

Nickname of Celtic defence in the 1920s.

'The Pope's eleven.'
Nickname of Celtic team in the 1950s.

'The five sorrowful mysteries.'
Nickname of Celtic forward line in the 1940s.

'The moment the IFA legalises Sunday football I will walk out.'
Captain Wilton, IFA president and a former UVF member, in a statement to the AGM (1927).

'What's the difference between a Taige B—d and a Roman Catholic? A Roman Catholic plays for Linfield.'
Joke after Linfield signed their first Catholic, Dessie Gorman (1989).

'What really riled me is that Linfield secretary Joe Mackey told me that Windsor was my home and that I shouldn't be over there playing with those Taigs.'
Jimmy Jones, a Protestant who played for Belfast Celtic, describing his approach from Linfield.

'How can a selection committee, containing one Catholic, select a team containing ten Protestants and one Catholic?'
Senator W. H. Wilson, President of the North West Football Association, on the selection of the IFA team against England (October 1948).

'When we had nothing we had Belfast Celtic and then we had everything.'
Bill McKavanagh, Belfast Celtic supporter, quoted in Padraig Coyle, *Paradise Lost & Found* (1999).

'I'm sure if I was a Linfield player I could have got more work as a plater in the shipyards. But it was held against me. That made the games against Linfield all the more special.'

Jack Mahood, a Protestant, who played for Belfast Celtic in the 1920s.

'Recent events have put a damper on soccer games in the north, and we hope that we hope we will be excused if we make no further mention of them than to say they are by no means forgotten.'

Notes in the programme for Belfast Celtic v. Distillery (6 January 1949).

'We are up to our necks in Fenian blood, surrender or you'll die.'

Linfield supporters song.

'As one raised in the shadow of Celtic Park, it's a depressing feeling to pass the old place and know its turnstiles are closed for ever to the football fans of Belfast.'

Charlie Tully, *Passed to You* (1958).

'Ten Yugoslav players attended mass in the pro-Cathedral yesterday.'

Report in *Irish Independent* prior to the match that Archbishop McQuaid wanted banned going ahead.

'It was a pity, both for the sake of Irish football and Irish life in general. Some of us have always had the feeling that a football match involving Celtic would have provided Celtic with an outlet for their feelings – they would have been

better employed shouting on the terraces of Celtic Park than throwing stones on the streets.'
Malcolm Brodie, *Belfast Telegraph*.

'Some of the Scotland team started to make remarks about Catholics and Papish b—ds. Naturally they were disappointed and felt they had let themselves down. But even so I was shocked at some of the things that were being said. I'd never experienced such bigotry.'
Mick O'Flanagan, Irish rugby and soccer international who played for Belfast Celtic against the full Scotland team on their last tour to the USA. Belfast Celtic won 2-0.

'It has been authoritatively learned that the Irish Football League has received a letter from Belfast Celtic Club requesting permission to withdraw their membership.'
Irish News (30 April 1949), the first hint that probably the greatest club side in Irish history was withdrawing from the game.

'The affair may have surprised any visitor to Belfast, but not anyone who is familiar with the state of affairs here.'
Anonymous letter (January 1949).

'It was all over in 10 to 15 seconds, probably less. As soon as the door opened I heard three bangs or bursts. That must have been 60 bullets for every bang.'
Survivor of Loughinisland massacre, *Irish News*. Eamon Byrne, Barney Green, Malcolm Jenkinson, Adrian Logan, Daniel McCreanor and Patsy O'Hare died in the attack carried out by the UVF.

'I didn't know it was high mass.'
Shay Gibbons, explaining why he is late reporting to the
Gresham Hotel as was the custom 'after mass on Sundays'
(1955).

'Mass tomorrow evening will be at 8 p.m., and 8.30 p.m. if
there is extra time.'
Apocryphal tale of Irish priest in Glasgow's altar
announcement the day before the 1967 European Cup final.

'The green garments were bad enough, but did he have to
hold the cup up at half-time.'
Punchline of joke about Rangers supporter who was persuaded
to attend a Catholic mass by a Celtic-supporting friend.

'I watched this wild and wonderful harmless celebration of
human beings just simply bringing out the best in themselves, just a parade of the best there is in human nature and
tried to connect it with the worst. Impossible, just impossible.'
Marie Jones, *Night in November* (1994). Her lead character
has just heard the news for the Loughinisland massacre of six
people watching the Ireland–Italy World Cup match in
O'Toole's Heights Bar in Loughinisland, County Down.

'For the last twelve years I have been manager there has been
practically a civil war in Northern Ireland yet my teams have
been a mixture of both tribes who roomed together, worked
together, played together, isn't it amazing. If the rest of society
could reflect that there wouldn't be much trouble in Northern
Ireland.'
Billy Bingham, manager of Northern Ireland (1993).

'Neil Lennon RIP.'
Graffiti on the approaches to Windsor Park before Northern Ireland's Catholic captain withdrew from the team (2001).

'They're not in my shoes.'
Neil Lennon, to critics who told him he should face down the death threats and continue to play.

'A lot of people are behind me. If what happened has made people think about the situation a wee bit more then maybe something positive has come out of a lot of negatives.'
Neil Lennon, talking after the threats.

'I don't think the Lord will mind if we sing a chorus of olé, olé.'
Priest, at mass in Dublin on the morning after the World Cup victory over Italy (19 June 1994).

'One Parish priest in Glasgow jocularly suggested that attendance at Celtic matches might be considered an eighth sacrament.'
Pat McGoldrick, *The Irish Times* (23 April 1988).

'Did you bless that post, Father?'
Player, who had just hit the post, to *Father Ted* star Dermot Morgan, who was standing in his customary position behind the goal at a match in Belfield.

'Will Ye No Come Back Again.'
Banner at Belfast Celtic selection against Glasgow Celtic at Celtic Park (1952).

'Most of the people I know follow the Republic.'

Neil Lennon, on how Catholics in Northern Ireland don't support the Irish FA team.

'Perhaps the time has come for Northern Ireland to move from Windsor Park.'

Ian Dowie, Linfield fan, on the sectarianism of Northern Ireland's supporters.

'Does that mean Belfast Celtic can come back into football.'

Caller to Talkback on the day of the IRA ceasefire (31 August 1994).

Saipan

Future generations will find it difficult to understand how, for a whole month in 2002 nobody could talk about anything else except the row between the captain and the manager of Ireland's soccer team. People compared it with the Home Rule question of 1914 or the Civil War over the Treaty in 1922. Not much was learned from the thousands of words of argument generated, but they serve as an interesting example of how a family squabble should not be handled.

'The pitch was like a car park.'
Roy Keane, making his most famous criticism of the training facilities in Saipan.

'The people of Ireland will forgive him but I never will. He is a disgrace to his country.'
Jack Charlton, on Roy Keane.

'Why didn't we telephone in advance and say whatever France had, we're having that?'

John Brennan, on the training facilities for the Irish team, *Sunday World.*

'You were a crap player, you are a crap manager, the only reason I have any dealings with you is that somehow you are manager of my country and you're not even Irish, you English c—t. You can stick it up your b—cks.'

Roy Keane, to Mick McCarthy.

'As he waded in with one expletive after another I asked myself, Was this my captain? Was this the man who could serve Ireland as a role model for our children? The answer was no.'

Mick McCarthy.

'What I learned from Jack: ensure that you're all inside the tent pissing out and get rid of any fellow who's outside the tent pissing in.'

Mick McCarthy.

'Roy wants the best for everyone in the squad. But I don't always understand his rage. And when he got on the bus and started staring at the roof I knew we were heading for trouble.'

Jason McAteer.

'Mick stood up to say a few words. "We go on from here now. We grow stronger from this. We stick together." And then he asked if anyone had anything to say. Dean Kiely is one of the quieter lads in the group. "I'd like to say something, Mick," he said. We all turned and looked at him. "If you want," he said, "I can do a job for you in midfield." And the place just erupted.'

Jason McAteer.

'Though my head is still held high, my ass is truly in the bacon slicer.'

Macarticus, when Keano threatens to leave, *I Keano* (2005).

'Packie said they'd worked hard. Alan said they'd worked hard. I said, "Do you want a pat on the back for working hard – is that not why you are here?" I did mention that they wouldn't be too tired to play golf the next day, and fair play, they dragged themselves out!'

Roy Keane.

'Finally, Mick [McCarthy] gets off a sentence. "Did you pick and choose your matches, Roy?" "I don't do f–king friendlies," he shrieks at Mick.'

Niall Quinn, *The Autobiography* (2002).

'I wouldn't send a player home but, if I would, it would probably be the best player in the world.'

Wording to an alternative Carlsberg ad, text-joke after Saipan.

'I can understand (well, no actually I can't) that the FAI can't afford to charter a plane to take us directly to Saipan. And I can understand that since September 11 security has been tightened. But did we really have to queue individually at check-in? And was there no shorter route than Amsterdam

and Tokyo? And did they really have to organise a reception before we flew out?'
Jason McAteer.

'He Came, He Saw, He Went Home.'
Arthur Matthews, co-author of *I Keano* (2005).

'I said to Mick that I didn't respect him as a player, as a manager or as a person. To be fair, I used the expletive against him as well, I'm no angel, but these things hurt me to be accused in such a way. The language was strong, but that's always the case in football, it's not a debating society.'
Roy Keane, recalling what he said to Mick McCarthy.

'I'm someone who witnessed one of the defining moments in Irish history. People talk about Robert Emmet's speech from the dock. They talk about the oratory of Brendan Behan, Eamon de Valera, Michael Collins. But Roy Keane's ten-minute oration can be mentioned in the same breath.'
Niall Quinn.

'I have never had to listen to such foul-mouthed abuse from any footballer in any dressing room or any meeting room. I have never witnessed such an attack from any human being in any walk of life.'
Mick McCarthy.

'Mick said some strange and very hurtful things at the meeting for our benefit. For the team's benefit. Things like, "You're just looking for an excuse for when Ireland do bad so you can say, 'Well Roy Keane was sent home.' And I thought,

We haven't really made it to the World Cup. We haven't really earned the right to be here. We owe it all to Roy. And Roy thinks we're shit.'

Jason McAteer.

'I love playing for my country but my sanity is more important.'

Roy Keane, on RTÉ's *Morning Ireland* after the row.

'I couldn't play with certain players any more. I am finished. The only way I would go back now is if Mick left and certain other players retired.'

Roy Keane.

'One line jumped out: "The players accept the things they do and that's why they're at the level they're at." I thought, "What does this guy really think of us?" I was disappointed. I felt let down. And I just couldn't quite figure where he was coming from.'

Jason McAteer.

'Roy has been victimised by the FAI, the Ireland team management and even by some of his fellow team-mates.'

Paul McGrath.

'Roy lives in Roy Keane world and refuses to accept other people's autonomy or opinions.'

Matt Holland.

'Ireland's Secret Formula: find an island with a red-light zone but no soccer pitch, go out on binges and send you best player home. On the eve of the biggest football tournament the world has seen, the Republic of Ireland squad appears to be behaving like a Sunday league pub team on an end-of-season jaunt to the continent.'

Daily Mail.

'It remains a moot point whether Ireland came within an ace of beating Spain on Sunday because the brooding intensity of their captain had been removed, or whether his presence would have pushed them further, but they proved that life was worth living without him.'

Steve Tongue, English journalist, *The Times.*

'There are wider questions than the conduct of one man. In the controversies surrounding Ireland's World Cup campaign, some in the media have come to see themselves more as partisans than analysts. They have lost all sense of proportion and objectivity.'

Irish Independent editorial.

'How dare this large, belligerent, bloody-minded English toe-rag cast aspirations on two magnificent men to whom he owes so much, not least the legendary status in which he glories.'

Eamon Dunphy, paying tribute to Jack Charlton after the former Ireland manager criticised Roy Keane and Paul McGrath on *The Late, Late Show.*

'I had to row the ship all the way here with wooden spoons'

Keano, complaining about the poor conditions experienced by the Irish warriors on their way to the war, *I Keano* (2005).

'We tend to get very emotional about sport.'
Eamon Dunphy.

'What would we make of an officer who said the conditions were so bad that he would not return to them in the future, regardless of what happened to his men? This is what Roy Keane did. This is what his apologists defend. And they don't know what they're doing, because they haven't got the loyalty DNA. They don't know what it is. They think that loyalty only really applies when the going is good, and that when the going gets tough, it's time to look for the escape clauses, pleading mitigating circumstances – that the FAI are a shower of wallies, the other players are cowards, that Mick McCarthy is a clown.'
Kevin Myers, *The Irish Times.*

'I'm not going to raise the R&M issue, in case I might be accused of starting a campaign.'
Marian Finucane. R&M became shorthand for Roy and Mick for a few heady weeks.

'When Roy got to Saipan he realised he didn't want to be there. It would almost seem like he did everything in his power to make sure that he wasn't there for too long.'
Mark Lawrenson.

'Roy of the Moaners.'
Letter to *The Irish Times.*

'I don't know why footballers moan so much, given the money we earn and the life we lead but we do. The training kit will be laid out perfectly on the bed and we'll moan. The pitch will play like Wembley and we'll moan. The food will be prepared by a five-star chef and we'll moan. But today the moaning got a bit out of hand.'

Jason McAteer, writing in his World Cup diary.

'Will the former Irish soccer captain be now known as Keane-no?'

Letter to *The Irish Times*.

'The more that Roy Keane and the rest of "the lads" can be seen for what they are, ordinary lads, the more a new form of masculine identity which acknowledges vulnerability will be allowed to flourish, and the better it will be for all men.'

Harry Ferguson, expert on male conflict resolution.

'It was supposed to be the week of R and R for the Irish team bound for the World Cup finals. But instead of rest and recuperation, it was all about Roy and recrimination.'

Philip Quinn, *Irish Independent*.

'When you weed out the nutters, it's around 80–20 behind Roy.'

Eamon Dunphy.

'Does Roy Keane think he's better than the rest of us? The Irish people put up with sub-par services every day, from slow, unhygienic public transport, to hippy-bashing police-men, all the way up to "brown-bag" politicians. Why would he have thought the FAI should be any different?'

Letter to *The Irish Times*.

'What is it about the Irish character that conspires to turn accord into division? Just when unity seems within grasp, the proverbial split occurs.'

Editorial in the *Irish Examiner*.

'I write this for the common man. I love the common man. I've never met him, but I love him.'

Dunphia, the journalist who offers to write Keano's story, *I Keano* (2005).

'Mick McCarthy's biggest mistake was to make Roy Keane captain of the Irish team.'

Brendan Menton.

'Am I so terrifying? Do the birds flee from the trees when I approach?'

Keano ponders, from *I Keano*, the musical farce based on the Saipan farce (2005).

'The Roy Keane case was fundamentally misunderstood by people who represented it as personal luminosity and communal values at odds, when clearly they were not.'

Fintan O'Toole, *The Last Word*, Today FM.

'I can buy you, I can buy your house, your family and I can buy that mountain we were running on in Slovenia during our preparations. You were a dickhead player and you're the same as a coach now.'

Zlatko Zahovic, having a 'Roy Keane' moment at Slovenia coach Srecko Katancec after being substituted in their opening match. A reminder that other countries had similar problems at the 2002 World Cup finals – like Keane, he was sent home.

'In the long term, that week in Saipan worked greatly for acclimatisation.'
Brendan Menton.

'Knock knock. Who's there? Roy. Roy Who? Oh well, that's football.'
Text joke after Saipan.

'You'll never play for Ireland… There's only one Mick McCarthy.'
Chelsea fans, giving Roy Keane a hearty warm welcome to Stamford Bridge.

'Roy Keane is magic, he wears a magic hat, we would have won the World Cup, but he was sent home by a prat.'
Song heard at Keane's book signing in Cork.

'I don't know about the others but, when I get there, I stare at the ceiling and think of Roy Keane. I can't help it.'
Niall Quinn, talking about his private night-time World Cup thoughts.

'Beware the men whose talents are driven by rage. These people are not in control of their own art, their own selves, their own lives.'
Henry Lawton, *The Times*.

Scottish Settlers:

Celtic, Rangers and Hibs

Scotland became a centre for large-scale migration from Ireland in the 1860s and 1870s just as playing soccer was becoming a national obsession. The Irish who joined in found difficulty being accepted by local clubs so they started their own, especially where Richard O'Brien's Catholic Young Men's Societies had been established. Hibernian, founded in Edinburgh by O'Brien's nephew Edward Hannan on the occasion of the centenary of Daniel O'Connell's birth in 1875, won the Scottish Cup in 1887 and went on to defeat English cup holders Preston North End for the 'world championship'. Their success led to the foundation nine months later of another club in Glasgow, to be known as Celtic. And when Belfast Protestant ship-workers arrived in Govan in 1912 to work and turned their affection to the Rangers club, the migration to Scottish soccer of a proxy war between Ireland's cultures was complete.

'We are catering for Scotsmen, not Irishmen.'

Reply of Scottish FA to Hibernian's first attempt to affiliate.

'Hibernian were playing more than a game of football. No other Irish organisation in any field had reached such prominence in Scottish affairs. Victory would be an affirmation of Irish pride, a chance to say to Scotland, we've really arrived at last, we are part of your country and we are here to stay.'

Alan Lugton on the 1887 Scottish Cup final, *The Making of Hibernian* (1995).

'Hibernian must be possessed of the greatest skill and perseverance to have achieved such a glorious result amongst a host of competitors animated not only by rivalry which is the usual concomitant of the game but, I am sorry to say, in many cases by a bigotry so great as to be a much stronger incentive to exertion.'

Dr Conway, speaking after Hibernian won the Scottish Cup (1887).

'What has politics to do with a simple game of football? God Save Ireland is purely a political phrase. Unless it is, as I have long suspected, that with the Green jerseys the destinies of unhappy Ireland seem to be wrapped up in the game.'

Letter to a newspaper after Hibernian's Scottish Cup victory (1887).

'The effect of this upon our own happiness will not be the only good result derived, for each advance will increase vastly the weight of our influence, and so enable us to render more efficient assistance towards obtaining for our country that which the united political sagacity of our trusted leaders has indicated as the first essential to her happiness, namely Home Government for Ireland.'

Dr Conway, speaking after Hibernian won the Scottish Cup (1887).

'Bathgate Shamrock, Cambuslang Hibernian, Edinburgh Celtic, Edinburgh Shamrock, Edinburgh Emerald, Edinburgh Emmett, Edinburgh Harp, Fauldhouse Hibernian, Glasgow Hibernian, Leith Harp, Loanhead Sarsfield, Paisley Hibernian, Partick Celtic, Shamrock Guild, Springburn Hibernian and Young Ireland.'

List of clubs with Irish names in 1880s Scottish soccer, Alan Lugton, *The Making of Hibernian* (1995).

'We do not believe in clubs formed on sectarian lines, it does the cause of religion more harm than good and it brings the charity and humanity of sport into a narrow channel for the outflow of tolerance and the coarse feelings of our everyday life.'

James Diamond, on the foundation of Dundee Harp, evolve as Dundee Hibs and eventually Dundee United.

'The game languished, gradually decayed and would probably have gone the way of amateur cricket and professional foot-running. The press did its best to stimulate interest in the doings of Dumbarton, Cambusland, Hibernian and Renton, but to city enthusiast at least, Queen's Park were the only club and when the amateur team failed to hold its own with the pseudo amateur, association football lost all interest to them. It was at this stage the Celtic club were formed, and football given a new lease of life. The Eastern club brought a new following to the game. Thousands who had previously never given a thought to football rallied to the new club, while thousands hitherto oblivious to the fascination of the game decided, for reasons of their won, to support the club likeliest to oppose the new organisation. Just as opposition is the life of trade, so did the rivalry, healthy or otherwise, between the new club and its challenger breathe new life into football.'

Version of 'How the Irish Saved Scottish Football', from *The Bulletin* (19 May 1917).

'We learn that the efforts which have lately been made to organise a first class Catholic club have been consummated. We wish the Celts every success.'

Scottish Umpire magazine on the news that Glasgow Celtic was being established (November 1887).

'With such an Irish constituency as that to be found in Dundee, we can imagine no better field for a first class Irish team and with the influence of the Roman Catholic clergy at its head, its sectarian success can now be almost assured.'

Scottish Sport on the foundation of Dundee Harp, later to evolve as Dundee Hibs and eventually Dundee United (1888).

'After I joined Celtic I was walking down a street in Glasgow when someone shouted, "Fenian b—d", I had to go and look it up, Fenian that is.

Mick McCarthy.

'On alien soil like yourself I am here/I'll take root and flourish of that never fear/And though I'll be crossed sore and aft by the foes/You'll find me as hardy as a Thistle or Rose/If model is needed on your own pitch you'll have it/Let your play honour me and my friend Michael Davitt.'

Poem celebrating the planting of a sod of shamrock in Celtic Park by Michael Davitt, *Glasgow Observer.*

'If I saw more Celtic matches I would forsake politics for football.'

Michael Davitt.

'They came from little Ireland/to Scotland's capital/They took the name Hibernian/The most Irish name of all.'

Song (1875).

'The Celtic spirit is best seen in the Kevin Barry which has been adopted by the Celtic brake clubs as their patron saint. And right well they sang it too. The best the rival male voice choir in the south bend could produce was a doggerel parody on a Salvation Army hymn.'

Man in the Know, writing about the 1922 Celtic-Rangers match, *Glasgow Observer.*

'Glaswegian definition of an atheist: a bloke who goes to a Rangers–Celtic match to watch the football.'

Sandy Strang, Rangers supporter, in Stephen Walsh, *Voices of the Old Firm* (1995).

'The curse of Cromwell blast the hand that stole the sod that Michael cut/May all his praties turn to sand – the crawling, thieving scut/That precious site of Irish soil with verdant shamrocks overgrown/Was token of a glorious soil more fitting far than fretted stone/Again I say, may Heaven blight that soulless knave/May all his sunshine be like night and the sod rest heavy on his grave.'

Poem after original sod was stolen, *Glasgow Observer.*

'Celtic is an anaemic club badly in need of a blood transfusion'

Newspaper criticism of 1965, quoted in Tom Campbell and Pat Woods, *Dreams and Songs to Sing: A New History of Celtic* (1996) – two years later Celtic won the Scottish Cup.

'Still the Scottish football ground is the place to go when you're half pissed, to urinate down the back of the man in front of you and to use the language of the barrack room. And among two legion supporters in this country, the place to go to sing those hateful songs of Ireland.'

Ian Archer, journalist, *When Will We See Your Like Again* (1977).

'The world of Scottish football was rocked to its pre-cast concrete foundations over the close season when Rangers finally broke with 100 years tradition and bought a player from FC Nantes for the first time in their history.'

The Absolute Game, on the signing of Ranger's first Catholic Mo Johnston (1989).

'For a time I did unite Rangers and Celtic fans. There were people in both camps who hated me.'

Mo Johnston.

'We are, we are, we are the Billy Boys [twice]/We're up to our necks in Fenian blood, surrender or you'll die/And we'll follow Rangers [Linfield] till we die.'
Enduring Rangers or Linfield supporters' song. The Billy Boys were a group who carried out sectarian murders of Catholics in 1920s Glasgow.

'I was born under a Union Jack [twice]/Do I know where hell is?/Hell is in the Falls/Heaven is the Shankill Road/And we'll guard old Derry's walls.'
1960s Rangers supporters' song, sung to the air of 'A Wandering Star'.

'I'm roaming in the gloaming with a shamrock in my hand/I'm roaming in the gloaming with St Patrick's Fenian band/And when the music stops, it's fuck King Billy and John Knox/I'm glad to be a Roman Catholic.'
Celtic supporters' song.

'Come along the Rangers/buckle up your belts/You'll maybe beat the Hearts/but you'll never beat the Celts.'
Celtic fans' song of the 1980s.

'It's a grand old team to play for/It's a Grand Old team to see/And if you know your history/It's enough to make your heart glow.'
Celtic fans' song of the 1980s.

'Bands? You ought to have seen them. They perambulated all the district until well in the evening. And with the aid of a liberal use of party music helped to make things hum along merrily. Of course this caused a risk of a ruction with Billy's men. But what of that?'

Scottish Referee (11 April 1892).

'I'm not a violent man, but as soon as I see the first flash of green or a Republic of Ireland jersey, something inside me snaps.'

Rangers fan, interviewed for the documentary, *Football Faith and Flutes* (1995).

'They call themselves Protestants but most just say that because they want to be different from Catholics. Most of them are atheists.'

Celtic fan, interviewed for the documentary, *Football Faith and Flutes* (1995).

'I'm a small, balding, ex-communist, Celtic-supporting, Catholic and Unionist. Therefore everyone seems to hate me.'

John Reid, Scottish MP, appointed secretary of state for Northern Ireland in Tony Blair's cabinet (2001).

'The best combination of Irishmen that has ever been raised in Scotland, knitted together by an unquenchable desire to do honour for the emerald isle, from which they spring.'

Edinburgh Hibernian, 20 November 1888.

'Far across the surf we can see the turf/That cem from the Shamrock shore/the team tripping out, the welcoming shout/We hear din days of yore.'

Glasgow Observer (23 January 1926).

'Oh wrap the league flag around me boys/On high for all to see/For it is the emblem that should mark/The Celtic jubilee.'

Poem in Celtic match programme (5 February 1938).

'It's bad for families, bad for corporate hospitality and bad for business.'

Fergus McCann, Celtic CEO, interviewed in a Canadian newspaper after launching his *Bhoys Against Bigotry* campaign (1996).

'End sectarianism, bring a Hun to mass.'

Poster at Celtic v. Rangers after both clubs resolved to dampen down sectarian rivalry (1998).

'When you are singing those songs you are not being threatening. You are singing about your identity.'

Matt McGlone, contributor to *Celtic View* (1996).

'Ach Rangers are all right, but they still haven't invented blue grass.'

Jock Stein, to Hunter Davies (1967).

'Celtic tapped into a reservoir of support which had previously been dispersed among the less successful Irish Catholic clubs of Central Scotland, the Harps, Hibs and Emmetts of the mid-1880s. An estimated 350,000 Irish had settled in Scotland and that ever-swelling community was desperate to be associated with success in any form.'

Tom Campbell and Pat Woods, *Dreams and Songs to Sing, A New History of Celtic* (1995).

'Never in the history of world football has a team created as many new fans as Celtic.'

Francois Thebaud, *Miroir du Football*, after Celtic won the European Cup (1967).

'Celtic and Rangers got on famously for a while. They were soon suspected, with good reason, of contriving as many meetings with each other as possible. It was this notion of the pair as a business partnership that prompted another magazine, *Scottish Referee*, to print a cartoon in 1904 referring to them as "The Old Firm".'

Roddy Forsyth, journalist (2002).

Songs and
Those Who Sing Them

When Christy Moore wanted to write a song about young Dublin people in 1988 that didn't mention guards or TDs or Church or abortion or divorce or corruption, he identified the major cultural event of the time – the 1988 European Championship. Songs have always been part of footlore, community singing on the terraces or clever chants designed to mock the opposition.

The ubiquitous 'Olé Olé Olé' dating to the 1982 World Cup finals, was adopted by Irish fans soon afterwards and has become identified with the exuberance accompanying Euro '88 and Italia '90, the 'Boys in Green' predates it by a decade while the Flamenco handclap, first heard at the away match against Spain in 1965, is now rarely heard at Irish matches.

'In was in the year of '88 in the merry month of June/When the gadflies they were swarming and the dogs howling at the moon/With rosary beads and sandwiches for Stuttgart we began/Joker packed his German phrase book and jump leads for the van.'

Christy Moore, 'Joker Goes to Stuttgart'.

'We all dream of a team of Gary Breens.'

Gary Cooke, Risteárd Cooper and Barry Murphy, *Après Match* comedy team.

'How did the Irish know the French anthem.'

French journalist, after France v. Ireland in qualifiers for 2006 World Cup finals.

'La la la la la la la la la.'

What the Irish actually sang when the 'Marsellaise' was being played.

'Who let the frogs out, who? Who? Who? Who?'

Heard at Ireland v. France.

'Come on you boys in green.'

Irish supporters' song since 1973, sung to the tune of Olivia Newton John's 'Those Were the Days My Friend'.

'Come on you blacks in green.'

Variation sung when Cameroon took a 2–0 lead over England at the 1990 World Cup finals.

'With Union Jacks those English fans for victory were set/
Until Ray Houghton got the ball and stuck it in the net.'
Christy Moore, 'Joxer Goes to Stuttgart'.

'What happened next is history, brought tears to many eyes/
That day will be the highlight of many people's lives/Joxer
climbed right over the top and the last time he was seen/
Was arm in arm with Jack Charlton singing "Revenge for
Skibbereen".'
Christy Moore, 'Joxer Goes to Stuttgart'.

'Who put the ball in the English net? I did, I did.'
Ray Houghton, giving a rendition of his one line song on the
team bus after Euro '88.

'Are you watching, Roy Keane?'
Irish fans at the 2002 World Cup finals.

'Ireland, Ireland, show them what we've got; Ireland, Ireland,
we can beat this lot.'
Team song for Euro '88 by *Sunday Press* writer Michael
Carwood.

'We're only here to annoy you.'
Galway fans.

'London-derry, London-derry.'
Song used by Shamrock Rovers supporters to taunt Derry
City supporters.

'We are Linfield, super Linfield/No one likes us we don't care/We hate Glentoran, Fenian b—ds/And we'll chase them everywhere.'
Linfield supporters' song.

'Nice one Givens, nice one Don, nice one Givens, let's have another one.'
Fans' song as Don Givens put three goals past the USSR at Dalymount in 1974 and four against Turkey at Dalymount almost exactly a year later.

'Nor-Way, Nor-Way, We'll support you ever more.'
Sung by angry Irish fans after Ireland drew 0–0 with Norway at Lansdowne Road in the 1986 World Cup qualifiers. Despite a great start Ireland finished fourth in a group of five, one point ahead of Norway, costing Eoin Hand his job as manager.

'Ooh aah Paul McGrath.'
Irish fans at Euro '88.

'Ooh aah Paul McGrath's da.'
Irish fans waiting for the team homecoming after Italia '90, when Nelson Mandela drove past on a state visit to Ireland.

'Ooh aah where's Paul McGrath? Ooh aah he's in the bar!'
Shamrock Rovers fans.

'Ooh aah, Graham Kavan-agh.'
Irish fans away to Faroes.

'Here we go, here we go, here we go.'

Irish fans song of mid-1980s, sung to the air of 'Stars and Stripes Forever', most notably after victory over Soviet Union in 1984 and by Northern Ireland fans in qualifying for the 1986 World Cup finals.

'Que será será, whatever will be will be, we're going to Italy, Que será será.'

Irish fans song sung throughout the qualifiers for Italia '90.

'We hope ye pay yer poll tax, we hope ye pay yer poll tax – la, la, la, la – la, la, la, la.'

Irish fans at Ireland v. England in response to a chorus of 'Rule Britannia' and sung to the tune of a catchy gas board advertisement current at the time (1990).

'Ceacuscu's playing full-back, Ceacuscu's playing full-back – la, la, la, la – la, la, la, la.'

Fans at Ireland v. Romania (1990). They also joined a chorus of, 'Go home and make your semtex' until one of the fans pointed out semtex was made in Czechoslovakia.

'Hello Johnny Carey, you can hear all the girls cry. Hello Johnny Carey you're the apple of my eye. You're a decent boy from Ireland there's no one can deny. You're a harum scareum, divil may care-um, decent Irish boy.'

Manchester United fans' song of the 1940s.

'Packie Bonner walks on water, doo dah, doo dah.'

Irish fans, after Bonner's save in Genoa.

'We beat the French Nil-All'
Irish fans at Stade de France, World Cup qualifier (2004).

'It's just like watching Carlisle.'
Cork fans to Roddy Collins

'Is this the way to Athlone Town/Roddy Collins is bringing you down/Is this the way to Athlone Town/The first division waits for you.'
Sung to Rovers fans.

'The Eircom League is upside down.'
Shamrock Rovers fans, in their relegation year (2005).

'Build me up buttercup.'
Shamrock Rovers fans.

'Does your boyfriend do your hair?'
Derry fans, to an Eircom League referee.

'Oriel Park is a bouncy castle.'
Drogheda fans in the cup match against Dundalk.

'Go home, to yer caravan.'
Sligo Rovers fans, to Galway United fans.

'Ye must have banned your home fans.'
Rovers fans, in Longford Town home ground Flancare Park during a match they had almost been banned from attending.

'We're all part of Jackie's Army. We're all going to Italy and we'll really shake them up when we win the World Cup, cause Ireland are the greatest football team.'

Team song for Italia '90 filched from the Scotland World Cup song of 1978, to the tune of 'Tramp Tramp Tramp the Boys are Marching', or 'God Save Ireland'.

'Where are you now Georgie? With those boots laced up the side. And that Irish shirt you wore with pride. And that picture of you with Mike Summerbee and bride? Where are you now Georgie? I dreamed of you dribbling past City's back four. And leaving Joe Corrigan fumbling on the floor. And the Stretford End singing More Bestie More.

Manchester United song of 1960s.

'So on came Alan McLoughlin,/To help get the score we were needin'/But within three minutes of him comin on/The shagging North were leadin/A brilliant goal by Jimmy Quinn/It went in like a comet/The Northern fans went crazy/All we could do was vomit/We braced ourselves for misery,/Our World Cup on the rocks/When the ref gave us a free kick/outside the Northern box./Irwin's floated free was cleared/but not so very far/and it landed in the vicinity/of our latest superstar!/My memory is of slow motion/as he took it on the chest,/He let it drop, drew back his leg/and, I think you know the rest/One-all was how it ended/as the TV turned to Spain/Let's watch them celebrating/Jaysus they're still playing/oh someone's bleedin' lyin!/What's the story referee/Is someone after dyin'/You have to blow the whistle ref,/Spain have to stay ahead/And I began to pray again/and this is what I said,/"Oh God I'll promise to be good,/I'll behave with much more prudence/ I'll take me hols in Benidorm/I'll be nice to Spanish students /I'll never sin again,/I'll never be ungracious/I'll buy every shaggin' record/made by Julio Iglesias!/Just make him blow his whistle, God,/just make him blow it please/Put me outa me misery,/just put me at my ease."/After what seemed a lifetime/he gave the final blow/And I joined a choir called Ireland/To the strains of "Here We Go".'

Declan O'Brien of the Parnassus Arts Group. This rap song was played on the Irish team bus during USA '94.

'Give it a lash Jack, Give it a lash Jack/America we're on our way/Ireland, Ireland, Republic of Ireland/We'll do it in the USA.'

'Give it a Lash Jack' (1994).

'In Italia 1990/When Schillacci put the ball into the net/We started changing, rearranging/We've a team now you'll never forget'

'Give it a Lash Jack' (1994).

'We've got cousins down in Boston/Don't even know our name/And the son of a curate in Orlando makes a claim/He's got a distant uncle standing at the kitchen door/Uncle Frank, how's it going, you're not distant anymore.'

'Drive It Jack', released for the 1994 World Cup finals.

In all 42 records based on the World Cup were released, using every conceivable cover version of the theme: 'New York, New York, so good we played there twice,' or the Neil Diamond-alike 'Olé, We're going to America.'

'Gerry Adams, Gerry Adams, Gerry Adams your MP.'
Chant directed at Linfield supporters by Portadown supporters, quoted by Jonathan Magee, *Sport and the Irish* (1994).

'You wouldn't score down in Jack White's.'
Song heard at the Leinster Senior Cup final between St Patrick's Athletic and Shamrock Rovers.

'Come on the Blues who never lose/But very rarely win.'
Waterford supporters song from 1970–71 season. Waterford drew eleven of their twenty-six matches on the way to the title.

Derby county fans: 'We want thirteen, we want thirteen.'

Finn Harps fans: 'We want one.'
Chant at Derby County's 12–0 win over Finn Harps in the UEFA Cup of 1976–77.

Tactics

The first reports of soccer in Ireland give a hint that tactical debates are older than we may think. In the 1880s, clubs were obsessed with whether the English tactic of dribbling was more effective than the Scottish 'passing' game, beloved of McAlery and the other pioneers of Irish soccer. Individualistic performances seem to have been a hallmark of Irish games until the 1970s, while the debates over 'give it to Giles' and Jack Charlton's 'put 'em under pressure' styles created debates and folklore of their own. Ironically, 'give it a lash', which was a phrase used by rugby coach Mick Doyle and not by Charlton, was also used to describe 1990s Irish soccer.

'Our secret tactic is to equalise before the opposition scored.'

Danny Blanchflower, on the Northern Ireland team of 1958.

'Maybe they are in bed, but are they sleeping?'

Peter Doherty, Northern Ireland manager, having been told that his team had gone to bed early while the Irish stayed up playing cards, during 1958 World Cup finals.

'When you played for the Irish team, you played for yourself first and if you had a good game you were in the next time. If you played for the team and the team lost you could be out and no one could hear of you again. Even Giles played for himself early on. But as player-manager he was half the team.'

Joe Haverty, on the politics of playing for Ireland in the days of the FAI selection committee.

'If things go wrong I'll do a few dribbles and get the crowd on my side and my advice to you is to do the same if you want to keep your place.'

Charlie Hurley, advising Alfie Hale, quoted in Sean Ryan, *The Boys in Green* (1997).

'The first thought of Irish players from goalkeepers to centre forwards was to play it back to Giles. It might have been soporific football but, as the seventies was the decade that taste forgot, perhaps in retrospective we were better off sleeping through it.'

Dermot Bolger.

'When it is the Egyptians' turn, they may think back nostalgically to the days when all that afflicted them from the heavens were frogs.'

David Lacey, journalist, previewing Ireland v. Egypt after the Ireland–England match at Italia '90.

'I wouldn't bother talking about tactics. I talked about getting the crowd on our side. There was not enough time to worry about who was doing what. It was pointless to talk about free kicks and throw-ins, so my talk was basically a rallying call and then, hopefully I led by example.'

Noel Cantwell, on the Ireland teams of the 1960s quoted in the Sean Ryan, *The Boys in Green* (1997).

'This club is very much like an Ireland team – we drink a lot and run around like nutters.'

Jason McAteer, assuring Mick McCarthy that he'd feel at home at Sunderland (2003).

'We inflict our game on people. Put 'em under pressure.'

Jack Charlton's philosophy, as incorporated in the team-song for Italia '90.

'To be honest I'd prefer the Irish style at Leeds and less of that overlapping.'

Gary Kelly, after Ireland v. Portugal (1995).

'If you can't pass the ball in a football competition, you've got no chance'.

Mark Lawrenson.

'Let me say here and now that I don't believe in tactics. There is an awful lot of rot talked by a lot of people about tactics and coaching. There are a lot of people who wear the lapel badges to boost their ego, take their holidays at Lilleshall and talk of the coaching manual as if it was a football bible.'

George Best.

'I was talking to my dad about it and he couldn't believe we were playing so early on a Sunday morning. The last time I had to do that was aged twelve at Home Farm.'
Richard Dunne (October 2005).

'If we do play a long ball occasionally, it's a long ball. If anyone else does it, it's a wonderful pass.'
Joe Kinnear (1996).

'Opponents used to come up to me during games and say, "Ireland do not play soccer, it's rugby." I'd reply, "Yeah, but we are winning 2–1."'
Mick McCarthy.

'One day somebody might pat us on the head and tell us we have got the game right.'
Jack Charlton (1991).

'Now Dave, hoof the ball out of defence rather than fannying about on the ball the way you do in Arsenal.'
Jack Charlton, to Dave O'Leary

'Nothing has changed in this game since I was a lad. It's still the same do this and don't do that. As coaches we over-complicate the business. I'm not a coach. I am an advisor. A planter of ideas. A sower of seeds.'
Jack Charlton.

'Northampton had devised a plan by which their outfield players had five seconds to get to the halfway line for a long kickout by their goalkeeper. When the ball dropped, they had invariably more players in the other half of the pitch than the opposition and, by heading it on, they were then in a position to trade on percentages.'

Jack Charlton, on how he used the Northampton team of the 1960s as a model, they went from the old Fourth Division to the old First Division in successive seasons and then all the way back.

'The irony is that Charlton's miserly style of football is a denial of the spirit of the people behind the team.'

Jeff Powell, *Daily Mail.*

'We like to strangle teams, to choke them to death.'

Andy Townsend, before USA '94.

'Jack tends to play backs out wide instead of wingers. That's great defensively, but offensively, it isn't good for you. They can't beat people. When you beat a defender it opens up Pandora's box. If two are beaten, it opens up the world.'

Billy Bingham.

'Around '82 we had a good nucleus, maybe eight to twelve players who could compete quite comfortably. But we didn't have any more. We always had players who just didn't come up too it. You can get away with one. But not with three or four.'

Frank Stapleton, on the 1982 side which was squeezed out by France on goal difference in the World Cup qualifiers. France subsequently went to the World Cup semi-final.

'Most times you get in trouble it is not what happens on the ball. It is what happens off it.'

Jack Charlton.

'We invented a type of game for Ireland that threw a spanner in the works of teams that played from the back. We wouldn't play the ball into them. We'd play behind them. They were confronted with virtually the whole eleven of our players in their half of the field. The more they tried to play out, the more balls we won and the more chances we created. It worked like a charm. It's very simple. The full backs knew where to deliver the ball. John Aldridge knew where to run even though he was new to the team.'

Kevin Moran.

'When Jack turned up in his flat cap kicking the ball in his shoes and with no memory for player's names, a lot of players wondered what had happened. I didn't take him long to turn it round. He doesn't browbeat you with facts and figures, he knows what he wants.'

Mick McCarthy.

'The difference under Jack was when we looked around for the right pass, and it wasn't immediately apparent, we didn't hang around. We played the ball forward.'

Liam Brady.

'Strangely enough, the whole world plays the same way. Even England came out against Argentina in their crucial match – and suddenly started playing exactly how Argentina wanted them to play. Long slow build-up, little possession triangles getting them nowhere slowly. Only at the end they sent on Barnes, and he got behind them, got them turning and panicking, and it was a totally different game. Too late, but totally different.'

Jack Charlton (1986).

'The way Jack Charlton approached the game made us difficult to beat away from home. We dug in, scrapped for every ball and pressed our opponents all over the pitch when they had possession. Opponents unfamiliar with the English game didn't relish the constant harassment.'

Roy Keane, *The Autobiography* (2002).

'There was no point in us trying to follow them and beat them at their own game for they had a ten year start. So instead of attempting to play the ball through them, I decided we would go over them.'

Jack Charlton, *World Cup Diary* (1990).

'Why do football coaches insist on not training their players for penalty shootouts on the grounds that nothing quite compares with the tension of the World Cup? It might equally be said that nothing quite compares with getting into the ring for fourteen rounds with Mike Tyson. This doesn't mean that you don't prepare for it.'

Kevin Myers.

'The only thing I can compare it to is living in a big house with thirty-five people. We eat at the same time; we meet at the same time; we train with the same bunch of people. Your closest friend on the team will do something and you'll snap the head off him. And then minutes later you'll be fine again.'

Jason McAteer.

'People who have attended Flower Lodge during midweek over the past few months have noticed pieces of equipment, namely barrels, crates and planks of wood, set out on the car park. I feel I owe an explanation as to what has been going on and why. The answer is we have been carrying on some testing and measuring on every player on the staff.'

Dave Bacuzzi, programme notes Cork Hibs v. Limerick (April 1973).

'What I tried to bring to the Irish team was sophistication and values. I was going back to the very basics of football. When you have the ball, be as constructive as you can and when you haven't, do your best to get it back.'

John Giles, quoted in Paul Rowan, *The Team That Jack Built* (1994).

'There was a lack of interdepartmental choreography between midfield and attack.'

Damien Richardson.

'Ireland play football on the second floor.'

Lithuanian player (1994).

'Unless the FAI got us together after mass on Sunday that was it. Before the 1957 match against England they took us to Bray, to the International Hotel. For three days. It had to be

something very special for them to do that because they
didn't have any money. We were training across the road
from the hotel at the Carlisle Ground. The grass was long.
There were no nets. They knew we were coming to train but
I am sure the poor old groundsman did nothing special just
because it was the Irish football team was there. It was like a
ploughed field.'

Noel Cantwell, quoted in Colm Keane, *Ireland's Soccer Top
Twenty* (2004).

'When Wimbledon hit long balls up to a 6 foot 2 inch black
centre-forward it is destroying the game. When Arsenal hit
long balls to a 6 foot 4 Irishman it's good football.'

Dave Bassett, Wimbledon manager 1989, with reference to
Niall Quinn.

'I'm not going to head any of those balls because otherwise I'll
have to shampoo my hair and get my hairdryer out and
everything. I did my hair this morning and I don't intend
doing it again.'

Charlie Hurley, turning down a proposal for some heading
practice the day Ireland played England in 1957. Story by
Noel Cantwell, quoted in Colm Keane, *Ireland's Soccer Top
Twenty* (2004).

'Will the forward line stand up? Listen fellows, there's no use
banging the ball up in the air and sending it long to these
fellow because they won't have a chance. We've got to pass
it and we've got to build it.'

Johnny Carey, giving a tactical talk when he was Ireland
manager as recalled by Noel Cantwell. The forward line was

Joe Haverty, Arthur Fitzsimons and Dermot Curtis. Dermot at 5 feet 8 inches was the tallest.

'Johnny Carey was the manager. He wanted peace and quiet. He didn't want to upset anyone. He just wanted to smoke his pipe and he enjoyed the game. All he ever said to you was, "Fizz it about, fizz it about."'

Noel Cantwell, quoted in Colm Keane, *Ireland's Soccer Top Twenty* (2004).

USA '94

The 1994 World Cup has become part of soccer folklore as much as its more celebratory predecessors in 1958 and 1990, despite Ireland's relatively ignominious exit when they gifted two goals to the Netherlands in the second phase of the competition. There was also a fractious debate about Jack Charlton's tactics and his touchline ban. Most of the action was off-field, as Irish fans enjoyed the experience and players encountered new challenges and tensions that were buried under the exuberance of their experience of four years before – all exacerbated by unbearable heat.

'Before we played that game against Italy in Giants Stadium there was speculation about whether I should be on the team at all, so it was nice to silence the doubters. I can remember floating the ball over the goalkeeper's head and I cannot remember anything else. I knew my wife and children were somewhere in the crowd and I ran over towards where they were. It wasn't till after game that I was told I did my little somersault, I couldn't remember doing it.'

Ray Houghton.

'We were bored in Florida, the heat and everything. I have never been back there since. Italy was different because Italy was a new experience. Every day there was a game on.'

Packie Bonner.

'We all lost weight out there. Packie lost about nine pounds per session. In Orlando there was an extra problem with electrical storms which meant we had to break off training. And it was very difficult that we had to travel vast distances. From Florida up to New York was a three and a half hour flight.'

Ray Houghton.

'After the Holland game I was selected for the FIFA dope test. I thought the travel arrangements and the midday kick-off were the FIFA dope test.'

Roy Keane, *The Autobiography* (2002).

'The finals in the US went ahead despite fierce opposition, and proved to be a resounding success. The organisation reminded us that the absence of fuss is the hallmark of intelligence.'

Con Houlihan.

'My reservations about Charlton and Setters, the lousy preparations, our primitive way of playing the game, all the bullshitting and back-slapping that accompanied this

achievement caused me to hold back. We'd got the right result despite doing almost everything wrong. I couldn't just forget it all and join the party.'
Roy Keane, *The Autobiography* (2002).

"Oh-Ray, oh-Ray, oh-Ray, oh-Ray.'
T-shirt slogan after Ray Houghton's goal beat Italy.

'The man who wanted to have Packie's babies now wanted to have Ray Houghton's. He was delirious.'
Marie Jones, *Night in November* (1994).

'On the pitch the Italians look no different to us. It was like playing Bournemouth on a wet Saturday.'
Jason McAteer.

'Playing in 130 degrees is exhausting, even for a keeper. People tell me I should be okay since I can keep a carton of water in the net. But I have this nightmare vision of me standing on the line, downing a pint of water as a 60-yard shot sailed by.'
Packie Bonner, writing in a Scottish newspaper 24 hours before his costly error against Netherlands (1994).

'No one gave me a red card or a yellow card, the referee never spoke to me. Nobody. Except that fellow on the line, and he was out of order. It was nothing to do with him. He was the one who should have got fined. You don't really know how to handle it and what you are going to do. Because there are so many rules and so many people making rules. The guy stood there, and he looked at me and I looked at him. And he came towards me and I said, "Have you filled the forms in wrongly?" And he went, "Get back, you're no longer here." "Have the forms been filled in wrongly?" "Get back." He said, "You can't talk to me, get back", and he pushed me. And that's when I went, "You're out of order, pal.'"

Jack Charlton, on his argument with the fourth official in Orlando.

'The humidity was so bad that when the crowd cheered you could smell stale lager all over the pitch.'

Phil Babb.

'We like Jack, he is a crazy man but we need characters in football. However he must learn where to draw a line with his behaviour.'

Guido Tognoni, FIFA spokesman after Charlton's touchline ban.

'When Jack talks to Maurice Setters from the stand, will he reverse the charges?'

Caller to RTÉ.

'We kept expecting bags or bottles of water to come flying down from the top of the grandstand and explode around our ankles.'

Andy Townsend, during a match with Norway.

'You f—king cheat.'

John Aldridge, screaming at the Egyptian official who kept him from coming on to the field for three minutes, with the open microphone near at hand.

'FIFA-fi-fo-fum, I smell the blood of an Englishman.'
Irish Press, on Charlton's touchline ban.

'I had taken four phone calls and put the phone down on Charlton twice.'
Maurice Setters, Charlton's assistant.

'Next time we'll play Mexico in winter and see what happens.'
Jack Charlton.

Gerry Ryan: 'What will happen when 50,000 Irish bums settled into the seats in 44 degrees Celsius/110 degrees Fahrenheit?
Yvonne Judge: 'Rumpsteak.'
Radio exchange.

'Our 0–0 draw against Norway may well have been the worst game in the history of the World Cup finals. The Norwegians looked as knackered as us. There was never going to be a goal.'
Roy Keane, *The Autobiography* (2002).

'The only Irish hooligan at the world cup was their manager.'
FIFA spokesman.

'USA '94 exposed Charlton's crude approach to the game. There was no Plan B, nothing. At half-time, when a real manager can earn corn by adjusting the tactics to meet the demands of any given situation, the great man offered nothing. Except bluster. And even he had run out of bluster by half-time in the Dutch game. Outside, our fans were still singing. They deserved better than another gallant loser story.'

Roy Keane, *The Autobiography* (2002).

'It didn't have to be this way. Our midfield with Andy Townsend, Ray Houghton, John Sheridan, myself and Steve Staunton, was well capable of playing the passing game. Gary Kelly, Phil Babb and Paul McGrath were all capable of passing the ball from the back. Sadly in the Charlton plan that wasn't an option.'

Roy Keane, *The Autobiography* (2002).

'The Taoiseach had to open a stock exchange link, Charlie McCreevy was promoting tourism and trade, the Minister for Industry had an IDA contract to secure, in all eleven government ministers and two dozen officials travelled, meaning we had more prattlers than footballers in America for the match.'

Irish Press.

'The Celtic Tiger was conceived on an unseasonably humid June night in 1994. Nine months after Houghton lobbed the ball over the Italian keeper in Giants Stadium, we started having babies again – and lots of them. Houghton's aphrodisiac effect outlasted his own fine career, and by 1999 – just ten years after Ireland registered the fastest declining birth rate in Europe – we were back up there again on top of the EU baby list. The explosion in family formation since Ray Houghton's famous lob is a sign of economic hope. We bring children into this world when we think the place is going in the right direction In general, children are the most conspicuous example of 'buy-in' a couple can make to a society.'

David McWilliams, economist (2005).

'Imagine what Ireland might have done if led and inspired by a man of vision and courage. This is not very hard to do: Remember Giants Stadium, when with the spur of an early goal, the players overcame miserable tactics to humble Italy. Gifted with one of most formidable squads in Europe Charlton squandered it all. In football terms Charlton has failed and should resign.'

Eamon Dunphy.

'The hideous embarrassment of 1994, when the men who triumphed over Italy in the Giants Stadium were humiliated in the Phoenix Park.'

Fintan O'Toole, journalist, on the disastrous Irish homecoming.

'FIFA seem to believe that Ireland are the tradesmen at their soiree. The backstage consensus about Jack Charlton's touch-line ban is that he was penalised for refusing to conform to party etiquette.

Fintan O'Toole.

'We returned as conquering heroes, Big Jack leading the parade. I, like most of the other players, had had enough. There was nothing to celebrate. We'd achieved little. The whole thing was a fraud. But nobody was asking questions.'

Roy Keane, *The Autobiography* (2002).

'I suppose I'll know how I feel when I return on Thursday and have to pay for my own Guinness.'

Jack Charlton.

'Saturday 18 June. We play Italy. The rest is a bit of a blank.'

Joseph O'Connor, in his World Cup diary, *The Secret World of the Irish Male* (1994).

Verbals

The best stories of verbal exchanges on the soccer field are either apocryphal or unprintable – and sometimes both. In the absence of microphones for each player (now there is an idea for RTÉ and Telefís na Spéire), they remain outside the zone. But the 'taking out' of opponents by direct assault ort, even more cunningly, by faint praise, has always been as much a feature of soccer as the late tackle.

'He's a legend in his own head.'
Johnny Giles, paying tribute to West Ham striker Paulo Di Canio.

'A boring old shite.'
Jack Charlton, paying tribute to Denis Irwin at the player's testimonial dinner in Dublin (May 2000).

'Roddy is from a good boxing family and I think he must have got a few punches as a young fellow.'

Dermot Keely, Shelbourne manager, on his Bohemians' counterpart Roddy Collins.

'By my calculations Gary Breen could be overtaken by a glacier.'

Harry Pearson, journalist (December 2005).

'I sometimes have problems against fast strikers, but I find it easy to play against someone like Morrison who is more static.'

Patrick Muller, Swiss defender, before Ireland's qualifier against Switzerland (2005).

'This fixture between the National League and Northern Ireland League is a jolly-up in Galway for the officials. Nobody knows who won the last one five years ago, or the one before.'

Roddy Collins.

'While George O'Callaghan may not be the most handsome man in the rebel city (at least that's the word on the street), his abrasive talent can be a thing of great beauty.'

Damien Richardson, Inside Cork.

'If Shamrock Rovers ever found themselves on the wrong end of a relegation fight then the rules would be changed to offer them a lifeline.'

Willie McStay of Sligo Rovers.

'If I was a fitter man the first smug looking Freestater I saw would be picking his Fenian teeth out of his boots.'
Marie Jones, *Night in November* (1994).

'This guy's an idiot.'
Eamon Dunphy, on Sven Goran Eriksson.

'Build a bonfire, build a bonfire, put Sligo on the top, put the muckers in the middle, and burn the lot!!!'
Finn Harps website.

'Why did Noel King decide to leave now? Did he think the journey to Donegal was gonna get shorter through the season?
Finn Harps fan.

'All I could see was the ball. I thought I had a 50–50 chance of getting it.'
Kevin Moran, on his sending off in the 1985 English FA Cup final.

'Pat Dolan failed to appreciate the tradition that almost demands the eccentricity in the front line of its football team. Patrick instead chose to emphasise the equally traditional but now rather antiquated dogma of Cork being better than Dublin.'
Damien Richardson, *Inside Cork*.

'Look at this, you'd be taken off in the Phoenix Park for this. There, get that, one for the seagulls. Even you could play better than that Bill. Look, he tried to commit suicide. I'm thinking of making a comeback.'

Eamon Dunphy, on Carsten Jancker of Germany.

'No disrespect, but… I would rather gouge my eyes out with a rusty spoon than have [David] O'Leary back as manager.'

Simon Jose, of the Leeds United Independent Fans' Association.

'I like defenders to be big, mean and ugly. Two out of three ain't bad. Are you mean as well?'

Ray Treacy, to an opponent.

'If Tommy Docherty says good morning to you, you had better check the weather outside.'

George Best.

'Mother f–king Theresa.'

Roy Keane, on Niall Quinn, who gave the proceeds of his testimonial away to a children's charity.

Windsor Park

The final qualifier for USA '94 between the North and the Republic has inspired more comment than any other match in Irish soccer history. It was an ugly and frightening experience for most of the players and reporters who went, and a reflection of how even sport can be marred by a dysfunctional society.

'You always expect a bit of tension at matches but this was different, an alien crowd, a bad experience. Our worst night in football.'

Mick Byrne, Irish physio (1993).

'Wondering why the BBC had decided to send Kate Adie to cover the match, we soon discovered the reason. Knowing little of the history, lads like Andy Townsend, John Aldridge, Tony Cascarino and Alan McLoughlin were puzzled. What was striking was that the bile wasn't coming form the terraces. There crowd in the main stand were just as ugly.'

Roy Keane, *The Autobiography* (2002).

'Hey Townsend, you Fenian scum, I hope your mother dies of cancer.'

Andy Townsend, recalling a fan shouting at him in Windsor Park.

'Before the game I walked out and the crowd cheered. It was slightly muted at first and I thought: I want them louder than that. So I went and put my hand up in the air to get them to cheer louder. I wanted the Republic team to feel the force of the crowd. I didn't want them to feel any sectarian force.'

Billy Bingham.

'This is not a football match it's a battlefield. It is not about who wins it is about who doesn't win.'

Comment by the lead character, a Belfast Protestant called Kenneth McCallister, in Marie Jones' play, *Night In November* (1994).

'It was bordering on the nasty at times.'

Jack Charlton.

'Unbeknownst to me part of my bench was arguing with part of their bench. I don't know what they were arguing about. Jimmy Nicholls was arguing with Maurice Setters.

After the match Jack and I got off our benches and I went up to him to shake his hand and he didn't shake my hand. He said something rude which I can't repeat.'

Billy Bingham.

'I think the strange atmosphere may have broken some of the players' concentration and the level of resistance offered by the Northern lads surprised me. They really didn't want us to qualify.'

Roy Keane, *The Autobiography* (2002).

'Jimmy Quinn capitalised on a poor clearance to shoot the North into the lead after 73 minutes. As he raced over to celebrate with the fans, there was a strange irony at play, for Quinn's family had been the victim of the same bigotry which was rife that night in Windsor Park. They had been burned out of their home in Rathcoole many years previously, forcing them to emigrate to England.'

Sean Ryan, *The Boys in Green* (1997).

'Trick or Treat.'

Chant by Northern Ireland supporters as the Irish team came on to the field at Windsor Park, commemorating massacre of eight people in an attack on a bar in Greysteel frequented by Catholics.

'UVF 6, O'Tooles 0. Mexico 2, Cry Babies 1.'

Graffiti on the Shankill Road during 1994 World Cup, celebrating the massacre of six Irish supporters watching the Ireland—Italy match in O'Toole's bar in Loughinisland.

'Jack was twelve minutes from going fishing.'
Billy Bingham, after the game.

'One team in Ireland, there's only one team in Ireland.'
Northern Ireland fans, conducted by Bingham, after the goal.

'Does it feel a bit like Deja Vu, Jack.'
Billy Bingham, after Northern Ireland's goal.

'They may look like mere innocent football players but as far as I am concerned they are representing the IRA.'
Comment by the lead character, a Belfast Protestant called Kenneth McCallister, in Marie Jones' play, *Night In November* (1994).

'Windsor Park has too much history. From shots being fired regularly during games with Belfast Celtic in the opening decades of the last century; to the violent demise of Belfast Celtic there in 1948; to the abuse which Pat Jennings has spoken of; to the attack on Donegal Celtic; to the night in November against the Republic; and now to this. Windsor Park has been a theatre of hate.'
Michael Walker, journalist, after the threats to Neil Lennon forced him to withdraw from the Northern Ireland team in 2001.

And the Final Word...

There are times, off the field and on, when nothing is required but silence. Fortunately, in soccer culture there are always those who will fill that silence.

'Okie dokie, we'll leave it there so.'

Risteárd Cooper, parodying Bill O'Herlihy on *Après Match*.

Index

Index

Index